UP CLOSE AND PERSONAL

Shank

Wood

Bergeron

In recent days Christian leaders frequently ask me, "Where does the church turn for sound and practical help in serving the poor — effectively?" Thanks to Ron Bergeron and Anthony Wood, I now have something solid to put in their hands. *Up Close and Personal* is not only a compelling, page-turning read, but it thoughtfully steers the reader around common mistakes and explores a fresh biblical approach to ministry among the poor. And because Bergeron and Wood speak from daily contact with the poor, they do not merely spin theory but spell out concrete ways any concerned person or church can make a real difference. If Jesus has given you a passion for the poor, this book is zip-coded for you.

Lynn Anderson, Hope Network Ministries, Dallas, TX

How often have you thought, even prayed, "I want to help the poor. I'd like to know them. I'd like to share in ministry with them, but I don't know what to do. I don't even know how to start." If you are serious, here is your answer. *Up Close and Personal* is an honest and challenging resource to assist us in embracing the poor. This is a "how-to" book with love and compassion. Nothing mechanical, all relational. The three authors have lived what they are writing about. There is integrity here that will be a challenging call to pastors and lay persons who want to embrace the least of these whom Jesus talked about.

Maxie D. Dunnam, President,
Asbury Theological Seminary, Wilmore, KY

Up Close and Personal: Embracing the Poor will touch both your mind and your heart! Hope and resources are here in abundance for those "chosen to tell the good news to the poor." Three experienced authors provide not a short term solution but pointers for a partnership with inner city people. This book is worth reading!

Harold Hazelip, Chancellor, Lipscomb University, Nashville, TN

If we are truly to say "we are in the midst of an awakening or a renewal in the Church today," we must be in touch with what the Holy Spirit is doing to bring the Body — especially those of us in the "white" Church in America — to an awareness of two great issues: (a) answering to the need of the urban poor, and (b) charting a course toward trans-ethnic relationships and partnership in inner-city evangelism.

Jack W. Hayford, The Church on the Way, Van Nuys, CA

The evolution of religious movements has been compared to the settling of the American West. First came the Lewises and Clarks — the adventurers. Next came the wagon trains — the settlers. Then came the developers — the thinkers. All were essential. Authors Bergeron, Shank and Wood have been adventurers and settlers in the movement to evangelize America's inner cities. With this well-written book they embark on the task of being developers.

Charlie Middlebrook, Impact Church of Christ, Houston, TX

UP CLOSE AND PERSONAL

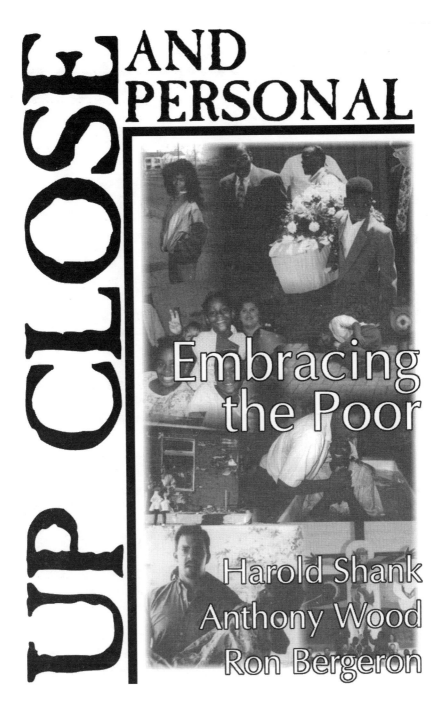

Embracing the Poor

Harold Shank
Anthony Wood
Ron Bergeron

 COLLEGE PRESS
PUBLISHING COMPANY
Joplin, Missouri

Library of Congress Cataloging-in-Publication Data

Shank, Harold.
    Up close and personal: embracing the poor/Harold Shank,
Anthony Wood, Ron Bergeron
      p.   cm.
    Includes bibliographical references.
    ISBN 0-89900-869-0 (pbk.)
    1. Church work with the poor—Churches of Christ. I. Wood,
Anthony, 1959– . II. Bergeron, Ron, 1958– . III. Title
BV639.P6 S48 2000
286.6'76819—dc21

                                        00-060240

Dedication

To my teachers,
the homeless of Memphis, Tennessee.
—Ron Bergeron

To Candi, Seth, and Naomi—
We did this together.
—Anthony Wood

To the elders of the Highland Street
Church of Christ, my companions in ministry.
—Harold Shank

Acknowledgments

This book tells the stories of people. Some are poor, some well to do. All are struggling. Most seek God, wanting to be his people.

As we look back on our lives, we clearly see the hand of God. Most of what we tell in this book would not have been done had it depended on us. He worked in response to our cries. He helped in answer to our pleas. He delivered in accordance with our requests. Ultimately, this book is an account of what *God* has done!

Along the way, others have contributed immensely to the relating of these stories. To the poor people in Memphis who have enriched our lives and whose stories we tell, we are most grateful. To the elders of the Highland Street Church of Christ, who have prayed for and encouraged and shepherded us in a ministry of mercy, we are deeply indebted. To Evertt Huffard and Wayne Reed, who have mentored us in urban ministry, we are grateful. Along the way, Marcella Trevathan, Allen Black, and Randy Becton have been key players in getting these stories into print.

These stories are true. In a few places, we have changed names and circumstances because we felt anonymity was important. Our hope is that these stories will touch your lives in the same way they have influenced us.

Table of Contents

CONTENTS

INTRODUCTION

Up Close and Personal: Embracing the Poor

An Essay

It felt as though God had led us to a precipice, to the very edge of the world as we knew it, and asked us to gaze across a dark chasm. With our feet only inches from the jagged gash in the earth that seemed to descend into nothingness, we lifted our eyes to what rose out of the mist on the opposite shore. From the haze rose a city skyline in silhouette, magnificent and ominous, blanketed in a shroud of foreboding as thick as the mist. Awestruck and dumbfounded, we almost didn't hear the voice. But we did hear it. Faint and weak. Distant and tired. We listened again. There it was . . . no, there. From all around, from within, we heard echoing through the city's maze a muted cry for help, almost a whisper, that said, "Come over and help us!" Gazing across the gulf from the comforts of a middle-class world, the other side seemed alien and forbidding. And if the abyss that yawned between the two worlds seemed uncrossable, it was not because of its breadth, but because of our own shallowness. Because the world that called to us for help was not some distant land. It wasn't the steamy jungle of South America or the alien desert terrain of the Middle East. It was our own inner city.

—Ron Bergeron

We never held mass prayer meetings in a stadium. We didn't organize grand marches to the state capitol. There were no radio or television broadcasts to reach the masses. We didn't have a fifteen-million-dollar grant or even a million-dollar budget. We didn't have a grand office building. There was no fleet of cars or service trucks. We didn't have a warehouse or a computerized database.

We just didn't have any of those things. None of those elements used in working with the poor are bad or inappropriate; that's just not what we did. We found that working among the poor was not a matter of programs or bureaucracies. The problem with helping the poor was not the lack of money or the shortage of food. It wasn't merely the difficulty of finding good medical care or adequate housing; of course all of those are critical pieces to helping the poor. We can't go on without them. But we found that one other thing was more crucial: becoming *up close and personal*. We found that helping the poor was just

One person at a time.

Face to face.

Hand in hand.

Side by side.

The road from the suburbs to the inner city was one of the longest we had ever traveled. Overcoming the isolation was the beginning of cooperation. Putting aside the insulation was the start of collaboration. Leaving our partisanship opened the way to fellowship.

We so often felt distant, like we were standing across the chasm Ron described. Initially, as we pondered the gap before us, it seemed that God brought us to this gaping canyon and gave us the *will* to cross but not the means. Or so we thought. But we soon learned something quite different. We learned that being up close and personal enabled us to embrace the poor. And that's what this book is about. It's about how God led us across the gulf and taught us to build bridges to the other side. It is the story of three apprentice builders learning step by step. It's about the questions of bridge building: How should we build it? To whom are we building it? Why are we building? Where should we build it?

On the other side, we encountered a culture that we admire, respect, honor, and love. What we discovered was a simple truth: *God changes people through other people, up close and personal.* It wasn't the "project in the projects" that promised lasting spiritual change but the quiet, persistent presence of God's family plodding along, step by step, side by side, with the people of the city. To build successfully, we had to embrace them.

Not just a physical embrace easily given and easily forgotten, but the interlacing of lives. It takes time in the inner city to develop a trusting embrace. Respect and sympathy can't be doled out like soup and sandwiches. You can't embrace the poor like some good-hearted grandmother welcoming her prodigal son home from the casinos. It's not convincing to either the grandmother or the son. The inner-city resident can tell the difference between head-counters and heart-comforters. They know how to separate the deeds done out of middle-class guilt from those done in genuine Christian love. They have an uncanny ability to see through the facades and hidden agendas that may work well elsewhere. We learned that, to embrace the poor, we had to be real with them. We had to respect them. We had to love them.

Sherry knew about embracing the poor. Up close and personal was how she lived her faith. She took care of twenty people in a small house. She took in both animals and people as strays from the neighborhood. Her house was always filled with the mentally ill, friends, children of friends, grandchildren of friends, and her own family. She befriended prostitutes and sinners.

Sherry's father had told her to "get a husband, not just a man," so when Milton came into her life, Sherry thought she'd fulfilled her father's wish. For the first year, Milton was a caring and devoted father and husband. Then he changed. Milton began selling drugs. And using them. Soon Milton's tender touch turned violent. The family car once used for daddy and daughter outings came home riddled with bullet holes. The weekends devoted to family time were devoured by Milton's increasing need for money and drugs. When Sherry felt things couldn't possibly get any worse, Milton revealed to her his dreaded secret: He was HIV positive.

When we met Sherry, she, too, had just tested positive for HIV. We were amazed by her tenacity. Nothing Milton could do kept Sherry away. She cared for him until the day he died. Once, before the end, Milton reminded Sherry, "I'm not goin' down alone. You're going to die, too." Milton gave her AIDS, but he never destroyed her spirit. Sherry never broke her promise. She cared for Milton tenderly, combing his hair when his hands were too palsied to move, holding his hand when the pain shot through his withered body, singing hymns to him when he trembled in delirium. Sometimes she would crawl up on the hospital bed beside him, carefully so as not to press against his throbbing sores, hold him in her arms, and sing one of her favorite songs. *"Soon and very soon, we are going to see the King. . . ."* Up close and personal. We learned what it means from people like Sherry.

After Milton's death, Sherry's own condition began to deteriorate. Making her own peace with God, she asked Anthony to baptize her. Afterwards, she tacked up every religious picture and Scripture she could find on the dirty, colorless wall of her living room. We still remember seeing that shrine as we prayed together with Sherry that her family, especially her daughters, now in their teens, would know the Lord. Before she died, she led two daughters, two nieces, and a friend to Christ.

Sherry taught us what it means to embrace the gospel. She knew that her time was short. When she asked Anthony and his family to take her home with them to let her die in peace, they accepted. Two weeks later, Sherry lay dead in Anthony's den. She had lived more righteously in her last days than many do their entire lives. Sherry understood what it meant to truly embrace the poor, because she had been embraced by the richness of the Savior.

Maybe you've been where we were, looking at the precipice, wondering how to cross or what to do when you reached the other side. Then this book is for you. You see, we've been there, and it wasn't that long ago. We still remember what it was like to take that first uncertain step. We recall how we faltered and how we succeeded. We know the kinds of questions we asked. We've already started our bridge across the gulf. Now we want to help you build your own. We don't expect it to look too much like ours. We hope yours will be stronger, sturdier, wider, and longer than ours, built with fewer accidents and setbacks. While your bridge may be different from ours, we're guessing that the similarities will outweigh the distinctions. We don't pretend to be experts, just experienced. We don't have all the answers you'll need to build your own bridge, but we know the questions you need to ask before you start construction.

In the first three chapters, we explore what it means to be up close and personal by introducing you to the people we encountered. We have changed the names and details to protect them, but the stories are all true. These chapters tell you why we sought to build a bridge. Then in chapters 4-6 we deal with the most effective means of embracing the poor. They serve as an introduction to the craft of bridge building. The last half of the book is more philosophical, trying to describe how our thinking has been clarified as a result of being up close and personal. The book ends with thoughts about where to build the best bridge.

We serve the poor because we sense a mandate from God. We don't explore that aspect of our calling in this volume. We serve up close and personal because of what we've learned from people like Sherry. This book is their story and what they teach us about mission in our own city.

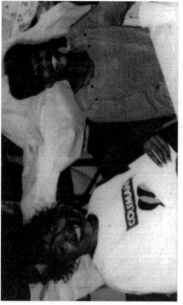

Sherry McNeil with daughter Toshua on Mother's Day
at The Downtown Church one month before she died

Downtown Church member Don Wright prepares
bags for food pantry distribution day.

Sherry McNeil with fellow AIDS sufferer
Tijuana whom she brought to the Lord

Laura Henderson interviews a prospective Life Skills student.

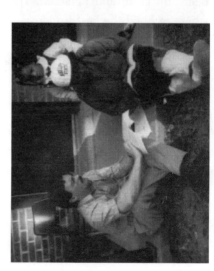

Anthony Wood shares the gospel with Teresa
in the Memphis inner city.

CHAPTER 1

Finding What You Always Wanted Where You Least Expected It

Christians in the nineties want to become personally involved in meeting the needs of suffering people. . . . They have begun to discover what happens to them emotionally when they are doing things that make a difference in the lives of people whom they personally know.

—Tony Campolo[1]

Have you ever found what you were looking for in the last place you expected it to be? I lost my car keys while raking leaves in the backyard only to find them under the foam anchor in the dining room centerpiece. I didn't expect to find them there. I reluctantly went to a party one night and was surprised to find an old, once-forgotten friend at the same gathering. I didn't expect to see Joe there. While helping a friend through a problem, I found some insights that made my life better. I never dreamed my health would benefit from his difficulties.

Jesus talked about the same kinds of ironies. Lose your life, and you'll find it. Moving to the end of the line is the surest way to find yourself at the front. Greatness is found in serving. Open your door to a stranger, end up entertaining God. Clothe the naked, only to find Jesus wearing your old Dockers.

Tijuana Mae Brown Was an Unexpected Surprise

The ironies of life. The city is full of them. Take Tijuana Mae Brown, for example. We performed her funeral. A cheap cardboard casket. Taped music playing songs nobody requested. Nine people in a run-down house that doubled as a funeral parlor, sitting patiently through the funeral of a person they barely knew. A burial paid for by the county.

One spray of flowers. No bouquet of roses from a loved one. No cluster of carnations from the grandchildren. No thoughtful vases of morning lilies from concerned neighbors. No obligatory floral displays from the employer. Just one spray of flowers.

Pretty hopeless? It gets worse. The newspaper report on her murder ran two inches. On page 46. At the bottom. An early morning fisherman saw her body floating in the Mississippi. Police fished it out, and investigators identified it as the remains of Tijuana Mae Brown. Homeless. Mentally ill. Now dead. Four days later the funeral. One spray of flowers.

Few of us want to think about such depressing sights, let alone be a part of them. But we found something we didn't expect at her funeral. Something that answered our questions and increased our faith. Ironic that we suburbanites should find what we were seeking at a funeral none of us wanted to attend. Sometimes irony is like a roller coaster. The long jerk and rattle-filled climb to the top is followed by the thrill of the plunge down the other side.

You've heard the names. Twister™. Cyclops™. The Slammer™. Plunge™. Wild Ride™. Those are names of roller coasters. The "I dare you" of amusement parks, complete with signs warning people with heart conditions to go instead to the merry-go-round and strictly forbidding anybody under 48 inches tall beyond the yellow line. Two-inch thick, padded metal bars clang into place, pressing the rider into the overstuffed vinyl seat. The clickety-clack dominates the climb up the incline, then there's a momentary pause before the 70-mile per hour plunge into the lake below.

But when you listen to people talk about roller coaster rides, nobody ever tells about the climb up the mountain. We never hear, "The mechanism for dragging the cars up the mountain worked smoothly, creating a peaceful sensation in my soul." Nobody ever says, "The car was painted a light lime decorated with lightning bolts of drab yellow."

Instead, we hear about the thirty seconds of being totally disoriented by the twisting of the mile-long corkscrew or how the water splashing in our face seemed to cut like a knife as the coaster hit the lake at seventy miles per hour. Wh-e-e-e!

That's our story. Not from the amusement park, but from the ghetto. Call it the Twister™ or the Cyclops™, but what a ride! Whee! The people gathered around the Blue Spruce sent us spinning. Their stories yet to come may thrill your soul as they have ours. The connection between Sonya and Clare and Lydia dazzles us to this day. Mrs. Harris's brief note sent us flying down the track at seventy miles per hour. Eric's story pressed us in our seats like Mach 1. Even the funeral of Tijuana Mae Brown turned our heads in a way we never imagined.

No amusement park roller coaster story tops these tales. Talk about going through the two-mile long corkscrew! These are roller coasters we'll ride anytime. We never tire of telling these stories. Wh-e-e-e!

As with most roller coasters, there were warning signs.

"Suburban churches should not start inner-city churches."

"White people don't belong in the black ghetto."

"Nobody will help you."

"It will cost too much."

The warning signs never stop the people who *really* want to ride.

The warning signs never stop the people who *really* want to ride. Like roller coaster stories passed around after the summer is over, we'd heard tales about inner-city churches reaching new heights and growing at incredible speeds. We heard about the corkscrew in Nashville that used 43 buses to bring 1,200 children from government housing projects to 33 different church buildings to be taught by 385 different teachers. The local mayor said he'd have to hire more police if it weren't for this church. Then there was the twister in Texas where over 400 homeless people gathered in a warehouse every Sunday to praise God. We heard about the plunge the mayor of Chicago took by saying that any abandoned, city-owned house on the near north side was available to a church that had revitalized whole blocks of the third most violent neighborhood in America. A church in Philadelphia moved at lightning speed in tearing down Connie Mack Stadium to build a church-owned-and-operated shopping center. The more we heard, the more we wanted to take the same ride.

What Area Will We Target?

We sent two men to visit these sites. "Your assignment: Study what's happening in other cities, and then suggest a plan for Memphis." They plunged into the work and, after three months, laid a forty-page report in front of our church board. After these two visited Houston, Nashville, and other cities, after they had interviewed government and religious leaders in Memphis, they recorded all their findings and boiled it down to two words: "Cleaborn Homes."

Cleaborn Homes: as one of twenty-two housing projects in our city, it seemed a prime spot for a new church. Few churches served Cleaborn. Another large housing project, Foote Homes, bordered Cleaborn. High unemployment, drug abuse, prostitution, and crime dominated that neighborhood. Churches in Houston and Nashville, congregations in Philadelphia and Chicago had entered identical areas with outstanding results. Cleaborn Homes seemed a prime target area.

Cleaborn Homes.

The board read and studied. They asked questions and pondered. Nothing happened. We seemed dead on the tracks. Like a roller coaster at the peak, the view was great, but we were getting nowhere fast.

We lived in the poorest city in America. That meant the percentage of families below the government's poverty line was higher in Memphis than in any other major city. We wanted to start an inner-city church because we had experienced the thrills of urban ministry on a small scale for several years.

Rowena Celebrates Christmas

One thrill we called "Christmas at Rowena's." One November morning someone gave us twenty Christmas trees to distribute to the poor. We thought of Rowena, who occasionally came to our commodities closet to pick up items she could not get with food stamps, like cleaning supplies, diapers, aspirin. Not all of the nine children in her apartment belonged to Rowena. Three lived with her because their mother was crack-cocaine addicted, two others were nephews.

After a phone call to see if she needed a Christmas tree, we loaded the best pine along with several sacks of gifts and Christmas dinner, and headed the flatbed truck toward north Memphis.

"You're a blessing straight out of heaven!" Rowena cried. "We didn't think we were gonna have Christmas this year!" That's what she said on the phone. Our first peek at her living room set us back. A four-foot-tall tinsel tree stood in the corner of the drab living room surrounded by brightly wrapped gifts.

Had she lied to us on the phone? No Christmas this year? "It looks better than what's at our house," we thought. "We don't have that many gifts under the tree." All those thoughts raced through our minds like the Cyclops™ on the back climb. It was like the awkward moment when the roller coaster reaches the top of the incline. Do you look around or brace for impact?

Rowena saw our confusion. "Pick up that package there, and shake it." It was heavy, too heavy for the shoebox-sized package.

"It's an old brick," she laughed, still smiling behind her tears. "Feel this one."

Something rattled loosely inside.

"That's an old shoe that I wrapped up."

She picked up a third package. "This one here is an empty coffee can."

"And that one's an old hair dryer."

We must have looked even more confused. Rowena laughed, dabbing her eyes with the hem of her skirt. "The kids wanted to have Christmas, but I told them we couldn't afford any toys. We decided to make our own presents, just to make the house look like Christmas! We pulled that tree out of the dumpster. We found the brick in the backyard. One of the kids picked up that old shoe out by the curb. The only thing I had money to buy was the wrapping paper."

Zoom! Suddenly we were cruising seventy miles per hour. We set the real Christmas tree in the corner, put the turkey on the table and spread the packages under the tree. Rowena sat sobbing in disbelief as the packages mounted into a pile on the floor. As we prepared to leave, Rowena grabbed our hands. "Can we pray together before you leave? I want these children to know who brought them their Christmas."

She didn't mean us. She meant God. With Rowena's five toddlers and infants cuddled on our laps and squirming under our arms, we thanked God for a Christmas He provided. We all cried. Cried because this mother had wrapped up an old brick to make the house look like Christmas. Cried because we had found faith where we least expected it. Cried because there would never be a Christmas memory quite like the boxes at Rowena's.

Wh-e-e-e!

The real thrills of life don't come from Cyclops™ or The Twister™, they come from helping people — like the ones around Rowena's imaginary Christmas. Sometimes the connections are hard to see at first.

Sonya and Abby Were Lost Then Found

For ten years Sonya worked the corner of Vance and Lauderdale selling her body to any man who had the money. Drugs and alcohol kept her numb. Fast money and a friend's spare bedroom kept her alive. Between having children and being in and out of prison, life went nowhere. Then Abby was born. Sonya decided things would be different with Abby, but she got picked up for prostitution. The state took Abby away to foster care and sent Sonya to prison. One day she bowed down on the dirty concrete floor and asked God to change her life. She found an offer for a Bible correspondence course in the trash, sent it in, completed the study, and gave her life to Jesus. When she got out of prison her Bible teacher arranged for her baptism and for her enrollment in a program called "Life Skills Lab." Sonya excelled. She started a Bible study in her home for others. She graduated from the Lab. She enrolled in school. She got Abby back from foster care. God had turned her life around.

Clare and Sonya Share Interwoven Lives

A year later Clare entered the same Lab Sonya had finished. Lab leaders remarked about the similarity between the experiences of Clare and Sonya. Both had done time for possession of drugs and prostitution. They decided to ask Sonya to be Clare's Christian sponsor. Reluctant at first, Sonya agreed.

One day in the basement of the Mid-Town Church of Christ, the Lab leaders introduced Clare to her new sponsor — Sonya. The two women stared at each other. Lab leaders became alarmed. Then the two ran, embraced, hugged, cried.

"What's going on? What does this mean?" The Lab leaders waited until the two women regained control of their emotions before peppering them with questions.

Sonya said, "We've met before. We shared a prison cell."

Sonya invited Clare to her Bible Study. Clare came to Christ. A year later Sonya and Clare helped a woman named Lydia come to Christ. One morning just before church, Sonya and her now third-grade daughter Abby checked themselves in the lady's room mirror. An unknown voice from behind said, "I was Abby's foster mom." Sonya turned with a jerk. The state took Abby away during Sonya's last incarceration. She had never been told where Abby had lived those two years. Now in the lady's room Martha met the woman whose child she had mothered. While Sonya was in prison, infant Abby was attending the very church where they would later both become members. Martha and her husband invited Sonya and Abby to their house to see the pictures they took of Abby when she was a baby.

So much of being *Up Close and Personal* is about children just like Abby. Helping poor children is an experience all its own.

School Stores Supply Area Needs

One night after church, several teachers from poor inner-city schools wondered aloud if the church couldn't do something to help the kids who showed up for classes with no supplies. Many didn't even have a pencil. How can you learn without paper to write on? Teachers, faced with dwindling school budgets, often bought minimal supplies out of their own pockets. Why couldn't we have a school store?

That began a long climb to a day in August. The teachers drew up a list of supplies that kids needed. A local store printed the list on the brown grocery sacks. Members took the sacks home empty, went shopping and brought them back full. About fifteen thousand dollars worth of school supplies filled the church lobby.

The plan was simple. Shopping was free. Children had to come with an adult. Over 240 volunteers set up tables, organized supplies and made refreshments. Others stationed themselves around the building as greeters to dispense hugs and encouragement. Each volunteer attended training sessions to help them prepare for the store.

As the day approached, we worried whether anybody would come. We'd sent letters home with the children on the last day of the school telling them about the August 22 School Store. We put signs up in needy neighborhoods. The local paper ran a short story on the projected activity.

Time seemed to stop the week before the store. Each day clanked by with agonizing slowness. As we inched our way toward the top, we wondered if it had been a good idea. Should we have tried something else? What if it didn't work? We closed our eyes and prayed.

The store opened at 9:00 A.M. When we pulled into the church parking lot, we saw children and their parents waiting in line at the door. The line went across the church parking lot and down the sidewalk nearly to the end of the block. They came, and they kept coming. Over one thousand children shopped that day, picking up thousands of pencils and giving us hundreds of smiles. All three local television stations covered the event. The local paper put a picture on the front page of the local section.

Wh-e-e-e!

It didn't stop there. We held a store every year. During the first ten School Stores, over 50,000 children received school supplies. They came from 150 different schools in five different states. That's 200,000 pencil erasers and 2,000,000 sheets of paper. Lots of happy kids. Hundreds of delighted teachers.

A few years ago, a grandmother named Mrs. Harris brought her three grandchildren to the store. Afterwards she wrote the director of the store a brief letter:

Dear Highland School Store,

I recently brought my grandchildren to your store to shop for school supplies. It was well organized. It was conducted with grace and love. I was impressed.

We have children in our housing project who know nothing about Jesus. Would you be willing to come and teach them? We can provide you with a place.

Sincerely,
Mrs. Harris

We've received hundreds of letters from people who have gone through the School Store, but this letter was special. Not because it was from a grandmother. Not because of what she said. Not because of her experience. But because of where she lived.

Mrs. Harris was President of the Resident's Association at a housing project in our city. Her official title was "Resident President, Cleaborn Homes."

Cleaborn Homes!

For months, we had agonized over whether to begin an inner-city church. For weeks we wrestled with where to plant a church. After concluding that Cleaborn Homes was the optimal spot, the board balked. The report was good. The thinking was crisp. The plan was outlined. But no action was taken.

Then Mrs. Harris invited us to the very place we had targeted! Wh-e-e-e!

The Downtown Church Begins

A few weeks after receiving Mrs. Harris's letter, a children's Bible study began in the room she provided. The children learned about Jesus. Soon their parents begged for a class. People turned to Christ. Then the Bible class for children began to evolve into a church. They outgrew the little room, found a larger facility, and took the name, the Downtown Church.

Eric emerged as one of the early leaders of the Downtown Church. Unemployed for most of his life, he drifted from one job to another. But in Christ he found something that grabbed his attention. He started writing hymns. The Downtown Church sang the songs he wrote.

Felicia Prayed to God and He Answered through Eric

When a local hotel donated $45,000 worth of furniture, the Downtown Church held a "furniture give-away." Felicia heard about it while walking through the projects. She came and picked out a nice green chair, but she was too late. All the furniture was spoken for. Eric witnessed her dilemma. He told others at the Downtown Church that they needed to help Felicia. We found some furniture, and Eric led us to the apartment where, through the open bedroom door, he could see Felicia with a phone, a phone book, and a Bible, sitting on two ragged mattresses on the floor. A broken kitchen chair completed the furnishings. They asked if they could bring some furniture inside her apartment. In tears, Felicia agreed. She told us she had called the rent-to-own places and had been turned down. Then she called on God, and Eric knocked on the door.

They carried the new furniture into the sparsely furnished apartment. The emptiness in her eyes concerned Eric more than the emptiness in the room. He gently quizzed her about her troubled face. Sitting on the newly installed furniture, Felicia told Eric she had just decided to end her life when he knocked at the door. She knew it would be soon, but she wanted to leave her auntie and daughter with a few things. She'd been depressed for weeks. No job. No furniture. No food. No hope.

Some time earlier, as the hot Memphis sun raised the temperature in her unair-conditioned apartment, Felicia had aimed the fan at her mattress and closed the bedroom door. Unknown to her, a man entered the apartment, raped her twelve-year-old daughter in the next room, and left without notice. Felicia blamed herself. She shouldn't have been sleeping. She should have left the bedroom door open. She should have locked the outside door. She should have. She should have. Then she decided there were too many shoulds and not enough coulds. Gun in hand, she was ready to end it all when Eric knocked at the door.

After Felicia poured out her story, Eric, an unemployed inner-city man, spiritual leader of the Downtown Church, amateur song writer, furniture delivery man for the church, got down on his knees in front of her.

"I don't have a job. I'm a poor man in a poor city. My uncle sexually abused me when I was a child. For a couple years I slept on the streets. But let me tell you one thing. I have found Jesus Christ, and He's turned my life around. Jesus is fixin' me!"

Every time we recall that moment in the projects, our minds race with thoughts of our amazing God. All the agonizingly slow moments, all the shaking back and forth, all the efforts that seem to take forever vanish away as God propels us down His track.

Christmas at Rowena's one year. The next year the long lines at the school store. Not long after that, Mrs. Harris's letter arrived in the mail. The Bible class, started at her invitation, became a church. Eighteen months later, they moved to a larger facility and called themselves the Downtown Church. Then came the furniture giveaway for Felicia. In May 1996 came the discovery of Tijuana Mae Brown's body in the Mississippi. Four days later nine people gathered for the funeral. There was one spray of flowers. The card said,

"For our friend, Tijuana Mae Brown. With Love, The Downtown Church."

The common theme in each story is not that we are great urban ministers. Left to us, the car would derail at the station. The common theme is the hand of a great God. We've found faith where we expected disbelief. We've found grace where we expected rejection. We've found spiritual depth where we anticipated shallowness. We've found God making connections where we expected nothing but loose ends.

That's why we say "Whee!" Ride with God for the thrill of your life!

---

1. Tony Campolo, *Wake Up, America* (San Francisco: Harper, 1991), p. 62.

Chapter One Action Plans

1. Find out where the government buries the poor and indigent in your area. Plan a trip with some of the youth of your church to spruce up their grave sites.

2. Read Romans 12:1-8 and discuss true worship to God in light of Rowena's story. Discuss how we are to be changed as a result of what God has given us.

3. Consider adopting an elementary school for one school year. Contact local school officials to find out which schools need supplies for their children, or ask teachers in your church.

4. Start a prayer list for the poor of your community.

5. Conduct an informal survey in your church to find out how many like-minded people there are who want to start a ministry to the poor. Look for potential leaders.

Downtown Church member Kasheena prepares clothes for a Clothing Giveaway.

Diane's boarding house burned with everything in it. Harold and Anthony helped her find a new place to live and get food, clothes.

Harold Shank helps Downtown Church minister Jeff Matthews load furniture for the poor.

Substandard wiring and tenants who use unsafe heating methods to stay warm in winter are sources of frequent fires in the inner city.

The homeless in Memphis often have no place to sleep but the street.

CHAPTER 2

We All Want the Same Thing

"Homelessness is a problem, but homeless people are not."
"To find a friend, be one."
—John and Sylvia Ronsvalle[1]

Most of us see the differences between people more than the similarities. That faulty vision robs us of what we most want. I see that he's black and I'm white. What I don't see is that we both want the same things. She's poor, and I'm rich. In the process we are both robbed of what we mutually value. It's not easy to see what we have in common. It wasn't easy for Ron.

"It's just over those tracks," Josh told me [Ron], pointing to a small road meandering between two condemned buildings near the south end of Memphis's warehouse district. Josh's body odor filled the small interior of my Toyota. A black, crusty ring marked the collar of his army jacket. His stringy, gray hair smelled of oil and trash. He looked every day of his fifty years. He'd been homeless for the last ten years. As we rolled over the railroad track toward his camp, he talked about going to the downtown mall with a "Will Work for Food" sign. But all that was about to change.

He wore a big, toothless grin as we pulled up beside an abandoned cotton warehouse. "There it is!" he shouted, pointing to a small bundle of clothes and rags heaped in a corner against the dilapidated wooden structure. "Here is all my worldly belongings!" he beamed. As we rolled to a stop, he jumped out of the car, bent over the pile, and carefully picked through his clothes. He rescued a small carving knife from a pair of trousers and a battered, coin-filled tin can from the bottom of the pile. "Looks like someone got my jacket," he said. *No honor among bums*, I thought cynically.

He picked up his "sleeping bag" — little more than a bundle of blankets and towels marked with the logo of a hotel chain — with a thoughtful look on his face. "I think I'll leave my sleeping bag here for Red. Can we stop by Third Avenue on the way to the hotel? I'll tell him he can have anything he wants." He laughed and spun around. "Ha! Anything he wants! I sure don't want it no more! Let's get outta here."

Just one week earlier, Josh received the best news of his life. After seven years of fighting the courts, he had finally qualified for his Supplemental Security Disability Income. The decision granted him a lump sum payment of $3,000 for every year since his original application — a total of more than $20,000! His disability? Alcoholism.

Josh arrived in court drunk the day of his hearing just to prove how little control he had over his disability. When the judge asked him when he last had a drink, he said, "About twenty minutes ago." Seeing his inability to stay sober for his hearing, the judge granted his disability. As a case manager to the homeless at a downtown mental health center, my job was to help Josh find stable housing, secure medical and psychiatric care, and control his money wisely. In one day, Josh would go from a sleeping bag in a train yard to a mattress and sheets at the Red Roof Inn; from drinking Mad Dog 20-20 to sipping expensive Russian vodka.

The Lousy System Can Make You Angry

I tried not to let my cynicism show, but as I worked with Josh, I found myself perplexed by anger and contempt. Anger at the system and at Josh. Revolted by the thought that my tax dollars had been awarded to a drunk, I wondered, "How could the judge be so stupid? Didn't he see through Josh's ploy? Didn't he see that he was just using the system?"

If I was peeved at the system, I was furious with Josh. Scriptures jumped to my defense as I condemned him for his sin. "If a man will not work, neither let him eat." "Lazy hands make a man poor."

My anger gradually developed into a lasting contempt. Contempt for Josh and for all those that reminded me of him: the panhandler on the street corner; the man with the "Will Work for Food" sign by the interstate ramp; the women begging for assistance at the church office. They were all like Josh. They betrayed my trust, abused the system, tried to get something for nothing. I despised them. Yet I was the newly appointed "minister to the poor" at our church. It didn't seem right. It wasn't fair. Why did God send me to people like them?

Working with Josh only intensified my anger and contempt. All that changed one afternoon in early spring as Josh and I sat in his apartment planning his monthly schedule. He had cable television, modern furniture, a telephone, and all the luxuries of a bachelor's home. But Josh hadn't changed. He was filthy, unshaven, and rancid. Bottles of expensive vodka covered the kitchen table like bowling pins. The apartment stank of vomit and stale alcohol. Josh's surroundings had changed, but Josh was the same.

My contempt for Josh surged. With the new advantages, couldn't he at least keep his apartment clean? He had the money to live decently; couldn't he at least take a bath? Didn't he have a shred of human decency? Determined to conclude my business with him as quickly as possible, I rushed through the agenda on my notepad. I just wanted to get away from him.

We went through the ritual of case management for a few more minutes, then something unusual happened. Josh began to cry. I'd never seen him show tender emotions before. His rough exterior and foul language had always kept a measured and welcome distance between us. But now – head bent over calloused hands – he sat crying in his disheveled living room.

I asked him, for the first time since I had known him, why he was unhappy. He looked up. His eyes searched mine. There was a long pause. "Do you really want to know?" he seemed to be saying. I waited. Then Josh began to talk. For two hours, he shared the sad story of his lost wife and family, his inability to keep a job, his descent into the abyss of alcoholism, and his decade on the streets.

My stony heart melted.

Josh panhandled on the sidewalks of downtown Memphis for eleven years. Sometimes he told people he needed work, hoping they would give money. Other times he made a sign on a piece of cardboard that said: "Homeless and Hungry. Vietnam Vet. God Bless."

Josh found little solace in the God proffered by local homeless shelters. He said, "The operators treated me and others like dogs." They served dinner after a mandatory sermon. "Soup for Sermon," Josh called it. Lined up in rows of twenty, stripped of their clothing, they slept on cots in their underwear, their clothes and belongings bundled and stored in a locked cabinet tagged with their bunk number. Corralled into the main bunk room with fifty other men, fights were common, sleep uncommon. The sounds of men crying quietly in their beds reminded Josh of the plight awaiting him the next morning. Awakened at 5:00 a.m., fed a scant breakfast of coffee and rolls, pushed out into the street – the whole process seldom offered any personal interaction between the homeless and the shelter operators.

After one night in a shelter about five years ago, Josh broke. He decided never to stay in a shelter again. He resented a society that treated him "like the invisible man," never acknowledging his presence. He felt rejected as business people ignored him on their way to lunch with the boss or business at the bank. Somewhere along the way, Josh decided he wanted to die. Since nothing mattered, he sought the numbness of alcohol. As his body cried out for greater doses, he found himself repeatedly hospitalized, seven times in one year. Once he waited a whole day in the emergency room before he saw a doctor. Twice, while waiting for treatment, the hospital staff sent him away, accusing him of loitering.

During those years, he found companionship with other career street people, fellowship among the homeless, and a mutual sense of victimization. But even that loyalty was thin-skinned. When Josh got his settlement, his friends wanted to ride the money train for another free drink. When he invited them to stay with him, they fought constantly. Their common bond was gone. They didn't think he was "one of them" anymore. "Life was better on the streets," Josh confided. "At least there I belonged. No one here wants me around."

At the end of his story, Josh rocked me by observing, "You're the first person who has ever really listened." Josh and I talked often after that day. I no longer felt contempt for him. We became friends.

Along the way, he taught me about those who hold the "Will Work for Food" signs. They won't. It's not worth it. But according to Josh and others like him, they will work for something more valuable.

I helped him find everything I thought he wanted. What Josh wanted more than his settlement, more than a new apartment, more than even a bottle, was a friend. When his tears melted my tough heart, Josh finally got what we both really wanted: a friend.

The "Will Work for Food" signs emphasize our differences. Their sign proclaims their poverty and reminds us that we are rich. They are the beggars, we are their source. They have needs, we have the money. Focusing on the differences keeps us from the wonderful discovery of what we have in common. Those signs make us do several things that keep us apart.

It Takes Going Far Enough to Connect

It's easy to talk about "the homeless" when we don't know anyone who is homeless. It's easy to discuss the "welfare problem" when no one in our friendship circle is on welfare. We cannot show great insight into the problems of the poor if we never test our theories on a single human life. We often judge a whole segment of society unfairly.

Often we offer advice to the homeless. If advice were all the homeless needed, they would have been housed long ago. Often we offer a handout. A change of clothes, a bag of food, rent money, and utility payments typically create chronic dependence. The homeless need what Josh craved and we all want — a chance to connect with another caring human being. After listening to Josh's story, I learned that I had deprived him of the one thing he needed the most, the one thing I was most reluctant to give: my friendship. When Josh found I was willing to listen to the story of his life, his whole attitude changed. Josh needed a whole person to share the burden of his fragmented life before he could piece it together on his own. He had to share his past before he could heal his pain.

"You want to know why I hate preachers?" Josh once asked. "Because all they do is talk. They got no more sense than I do, but they think they know everything." Josh struck a nerve. I often gave more advice than solace. He wasn't interested in what I knew until he sensed that I cared. One inner-city worker said, "You can't show your concern with money. That puts you in the category of a sucker, an easy mark, a rube, a resource to be exploited, not a living, breathing, compassionate human being."

We earn the right to be heard. We show our concern by giving our time. We ask to hear their story, not the one about losing their wallet on the bus and needing a few dollars, but the *real* story, the story of their life. At first, they don't believe we really care. No one has probably asked them that before. Giving them room shows respect, a rare and highly prized commodity on the streets. The more we invest, the more we'll learn. We'll establish a relationship with them. When the time comes for us to speak, they're more inclined to listen.

Listening breaks down the barriers and reveals our similarities. When I really started to listen to Josh, I found my anger and frustration melted away, I felt more at peace with myself. As I listened my way into friendship, I felt a peace that I had seldom known before. Not the temporary self-satisfaction of having paid a poor person's utility bill or the momentary thrill of buying supper for a homeless man, but the deep satisfaction of connecting with another human being and discovering that he, too, sought hope.

It's People, Not Programs!

Most people like Josh can get free food, clothing, and shelter at many places, but few places offer a connection with a compassionate person. "Compassion" comes from two Latin words meaning to "suffer with." Giving to the poor without feeling their hurt falls short of true compassion.

Novelist Leo Tolstoy tried to rid Moscow of the poor by giving money to beggars in the worst sections of Moscow. The experience soured Tolstoy. He gave to people who only "needed money to buy a railway ticket home," but felt cheated when he later spotted them still in town. Next he organized the Moscow census to seek out the "truly" needy. Yet his list didn't advance his cause. He concluded, "Of all the people I noted down, I really helped none. . . . I did not find any unfortunates who could be made fortunate by the mere gift of money."

Tolstoy organized programs but never connected with people. Most poor people need other people, not expanded programs. God uses people to help other people. Andrew introduced Peter. Ananias taught Saul. Paul mentored Timothy. Since God uses people to reach other people, we shouldn't be surprised at its effectiveness in our lives. If we meet them where they are, we can be used by God to lead them out of bondage. Clothing closets and food giveaways work most effectively when they provide a connection between two people.

The Currency of the Inner City Has a Name

Will poor people work for food? Maybe. Sometimes. But there's another commodity traded on the streets of the inner city. With money in short supply, most poor communities develop an alternative currency system. It's called respect. That's what kept Josh and me apart. I didn't respect him. He didn't respect me. Only after months of working with him and an intense afternoon of listening to him did we exchange respect. Once we did, our individual bank accounts grew, and we both prospered.

In the eyes of poor people, respect is a valuable commodity. Here's how Josh and others have explained it to me. Respect comes from several sources. The number of agencies serving a poor person is more significant than the amount of money or goods he gets from them. 1) How others treat you is a source of respect. Lives are snuffed out because someone "dissed" or disrespected another. 2) Respect is *not* automatically granted based on one's social standing, color, gender, age, or credentials. 3) Respect is based on how one behaves in critical situations. 4) Respect takes time to earn. Inner-city people know talk is not only cheap, it's *free* and often filled with lies. A weekly hour-long Bible study or giveaway is not enough time for most inner-city folks to understand a person from the suburbs. They respect those who prove themselves over time to be worthy of it.

Automatic respect is suspect. The average suburbanite is far too anxious to give respect the receiver hasn't earned and that they have no right to give. Tell a man on the street that you respect him, and he pegs you as a liar and unworthy of trust. Watch what others do, see how they live, and listen to their talk. Then offer respect.

Over coffee one day, one of our inner-city workers said,

> The man standing on the street corner seems to want pity, but he only wants money. He doesn't need or want pity. If you don't believe this, just try offering him your pity without your money. You'll probably get dressed down in a very colorful usage of the English language, or you'll get a contemptuous glare, or the silent brush off.

About every month or so, I run into an old friend like "Josh." Some have returned to their old ways. Some have radically changed their lives. Regardless of their current status, our friendship endures. We enjoy a mutual respect. They ask about my family. I ask about theirs. We talk about our hopes and fears. With many, I leave with a huge sense of satisfaction. I realize that my friendship and my respect played a small part in one person's leaving a life of crime and reuniting with his wife and family, and a minor role in a battered woman's regaining her family and respect. I may not be the only one listening and showing respect, but I'm part of a network of people who have changed lives in our community.

This deeper kind of respect comes most easily when churches sponsor long-term efforts to help the poor. We've established four ministries that allow Memphis Christians to develop long-term relationships:

1) A job training program called the "Life Skills Lab."
2) A long-term housing and counseling ministry called "HOME."
3) A church planting effort called "Memphis Urban Ministry."
4) A prison ministry for those just released from jail called "BARS."

Our relationship with a poor person changes quickly by moving the conversation to long-term help. We've often found ourselves saying, "Yes, we can give you the $35.97 for your utility bill, but we can also teach you how to pay your own way. Let us tell you about the Life Skills Lab." Many Memphis Christians carry business cards giving the phone numbers of these four ministries. As we encounter people like Josh with "Will Work for Food" signs, we try to move the conversation beyond the pennies in the pot to the means of freeing them from the culture of poverty.

People like Josh live in all our cities. Sometimes all it takes is a few moments of listening to their stories to melt a stony heart and change a life. The surprises that God has in store for you and your church will never be discovered until you take that first step.

---

1. John and Sylvia Ronsvalle, *The Poor Have Faces* (Grand Rapids: Baker, 1991), pp. 130, 136.

Chapter Two Action Plans

1. While giving spare change to panhandlers, sit down with them and ask them to "tell you their story."

2. Find out from the local police department where the homeless congregate.

3. Volunteer at a homeless shelter.

4. Spend an afternoon observing a courtroom. Take notes on the kinds of people that appear.

5. Have some business cards made that you can give to homeless people listing your name, your church address, and other contact numbers they can call for help.

CHAPTER 3

A Little Information Clears Up Some Big Misconceptions

"Stop judging who is worthy of a comfortable life."
—Noah Snider[1]

Misconceptions Abound about Homelessness

Have you ever discovered that what you *thought* was true wasn't true at all? The lady down the street wasn't ignoring me, she was simply deaf. The book I thought John had borrowed and not returned was in the box under the stairs. Bill didn't forget our appointment, but he had a fender bender on the way.

Most of us have a whole bucketful of beliefs about inner-city people. Mention the word "homeless," and a certain set of "truths" come to mind. Many of these "truths" aren't true at all. When the truth becomes clear, everything changes.

Visitors to downtown Dallas in the fall of 1984 probably saw the man. Unshaven, bad-smelling, hair matted, dressed in rags. He waited outside the Salvation Army shelter for the evening meal. Earlier he stood with panhandlers who begged a few coins from the tourists near the site of the Kennedy assassination.

His name is Charles Landreth. He's a preacher.

A homeless preacher?

Not exactly. Charles worked with a Dallas inner-city ministry. Touched by the plight of the poor, he spent a month on the streets, dressed like a homeless man, with no money or credit cards, experiencing life in the concrete canyons of urban America.

Most of us don't have that "luxury." For fear or lack of time, we'll never sleep on Main Street or in an abandoned factory. Our experience with the homeless comes via Peter Jennings or while waiting in line at a downtown theater.

But when we think about the poor, the homeless top the list. At least they did for us. Start with the poorest. We planned to use an old church building with attached parsonage as a shelter. Only a mile from downtown, just a few blocks from one of the city's twenty-two housing projects, and within walking distance of a health clinic for the working poor, the complex seemed perfect. The converted parsonage provided dormitory space. Designers offered to convert the auditorium into a multi-purpose room for serving food or conducting services. We were sure God was leading us to open a mission-style shelter for the homeless.

Then doors slammed shut. Neighbors of the old church building protested. Church leaders wondered out loud if a shelter was wise. Estimated remodeling costs soared. A tardy investigation revealed an oversupply of shelter beds. In comparison to other inequities, the city didn't need a shelter. We never unlocked the doors to the old church building, but the experience opened our minds.

We Discovered Five Levels of Homelessness

We learned that homelessness exists on several levels. It was our first lesson in urban ministry to the desperately poor. We thought Charles Landreth's experience on downtown streets defined homelessness, but we soon discovered five different levels of homelessness in our own inner city. The homeless in Memphis are not a single, homogeneous group.

First, many people in our city live in government-funded projects. Built mostly in the 1950s, these projects feature one- to four-bedroom apartments arranged in army barracks-style around open courtyards. Once the pride of the community, the facilities now suffer from inferior maintenance and a dispirited population, yet six thousand people are waiting in line for a project home. Until recently, the best way for a single mother with children to get a government-subsidized apartment was to become homeless, go to an emergency shelter, and finally to the projects. Homeless women with children are bumped to the top of the two-year waiting list.

Led by matriarchs with many children, these low-income project dwellers are homeless in a unique sense. They have a kitchen and bathroom, doors that lock, a mailbox, yet of the hundreds of project dwellers we've met, few live in the projects by choice. They do not want to live there. While they have a roof and a door key, they live without any real sense of ownership. They know a minor rent infraction or a daytime squabble with the manager can lead to the streets that night. They've got a roof, but no roots. They have a house, but no home.

Despite wanting a better place to live, many remain in the projects for years. Thirty-five-year-old Tamieka was born in the projects. A few years ago, her sixty-year-old mother fell off the front porch into the mud after suffering a heart attack. Neighbors gathered around her lifeless body. Some mocked the family's misfortune. Others cried with them. Tamieka took over the house, raising a third generation of the same family in the same project apartment. Tamieka, poor, dependent, and despondent, may well live in the projects until she dies, homeless in an emotional sense.

A second group lives in run-down substandard housing around the projects. These families sometimes own the houses, which seems to remove them from the ranks of the homeless. Yet, whether owning or renting, they often find themselves more trapped than project dwellers. Folks in the projects can leave their low-rent apartments at the first window of opportunity. The substandard housing of the homeowners serves as a ball and chain around their legs. They have few opportunities for advancement, and when an opening comes, they pass it by because they can't escape the property they own. While an occasional project dweller can, through good fortune, save enough for a down payment on a house, those who own their own homes in the poor neighborhoods face the hurdle of selling devalued property before being able to move up.

The Jacksons live across the street from a government housing development in a pre-20th-century townhouse given to them by Mrs. Jackson's aunt. Fallen plaster reveals the ancient framing timbers. The smells of stale cigarette smoke and poorly ventilated gas heaters fill every room. Mice and roaches live with the thirteen members of the Jackson household. With no money for repairs, they will never escape their house. It's a prison, keeping them permanently in the underclass.

The first two categories of people in our inner city are not physically homeless, but they could easily become homeless. Robbery, fire, or trouble with the law can change everything overnight. Inner-city residents live with the sense that nothing is really permanent. Both project dwellers and the poor renters and homeowners around the projects live on the edge of homelessness, unhappy and dissatisfied with their housing, living in fear that next month will bring an end to the housing they despise, but dare not lose.

Inner-city residents live with the sense that nothing is really permanent.

When people use the term "homeless," they usually refer to one of the following three categories: boarding house residents, street people, and transients.

Boarding house residents, mostly men, are the third category. With little or no income, they steal, panhandle, sell drugs, or work sporadically at "day labor" pools for money. At night, these men pay exorbitant rates for shabby, one-room, roach-infested, temporary housing.

Robert walks the homeless track, a routine of eating breakfast at the rescue mission, picking up used clothing at an inner-city outreach ministry, eating a peanut butter sandwich at St. Patrick's Catholic Church for lunch, listening to seventies rock music at the public library all afternoon before joining the 4:00 soup line at St. John's Methodist. After Prayer Meeting at the Downtown Church of Christ, Robert locks himself in the boarding house to guard his few possessions through the night. He stays in a boarding house for three weeks to a year before moving on to another room in another house. With permanence comes familiarity, and with familiarity comes danger. He leaves to escape the other panhandlers who know where he lives and constantly bum cigarettes or ask to stay the night. When he moves, the cycle moves with him. At age 45, Robert has no permanent address, no place to call home.

The fourth category includes street people who conduct their affairs at night. Memphis has two distinct inner-city cultures. One lives during the daylight hours, the other walks the streets at night. These are the dope dealers, prostitutes, teenage runaways, and gang members. Many who participate in this violent and dangerous night culture qualify as homeless.

Eunice lives with Earle, sleeping in his boarding house room in return for sexual favors. At night, Eunice works as a prostitute, earning money to buy Earle's food and a few things for her children who are in state custody. When Earle tires of Eunice, she will be looking for another "Earle" to provide her a temporary shelter from the city streets. Eunice's home is the street, but she gets to sleep with a roof over her head.

Finally, the transients, stereotypically called "bums" or "hobos," make up the fifth category. Back in the fifties, the lives of these individuals were trivialized and sometimes glamorized by popular clowns like Red Skelton. Norman Rockwell painted several pictures of the happy, carefree hobo, but there is nothing glamorous or carefree about this life. Some freeze to death every winter in the midst of our sprawling metropolitan jungles, sleeping outdoors by railroad tracks or living near the river where they fish for dinner. They frequent the shelters only on the coldest nights. Some sleep during the day because at night they become the target of roving gangs. Most die young. Many of them won't live to be sixty.

Earnest, who died in 1992, spent the last thirty years of his life on the street. The police found him in a trash bin next to the Regional Medical Center, fifty feet from the finest emergency room in the city, dead from a cerebral hemorrhage. It could have been detected if someone had known he was in pain.

More than the first four categories, these people are truly homeless, with no mattresses under their bodies or roofs over their heads. Perhaps saddest of all, they have no one who cares.

The nature of the homeless varies from city to city. Not all homeless men and women face the same circumstances. Not all need the same kind of help. Although we never opened the shelter, our work with all five levels of homeless people has intrigued us at every turn. We've learned some things about the homeless without joining Charles Landreth on the streets of Dallas.

Most Homeless People Have Plenty of Food to Eat

It sounds insensitive, even ungodly to say. We don't even want to put it in print as it seems to contradict all we read and hear. But we've found that if a homeless person goes hungry in Memphis, it's his own fault. People die of starvation and malnutrition in our city not because food, even free nutritious food, is unavailable, but because people do not know how to get it.

The vast stores of available food became apparent to us one day when we "walked the track" with Robert, visiting all the spots that provide food. Homeless people call it the "corridor," the line of rich people giving away food. In one afternoon, we discovered twenty-five different places offering free food. One place gave out mounds of sandwiches. Another handed out sacks of vegetables. Some offered hot meals.

The Holy Apostles Soup Kitchen in Manhattan serves one thousand people every day at noon. Most of the diners are men, eating a nutritious meal in the congregation's sanctuary. The volunteer director told us many homeless people in New York City will not accept free food if they sense any attempt to invade their privacy. They would starve before they would register at Holy Apostles. As a result, the soup kitchen takes no names.

The issue is in the *heart*, not the stomach.

The Holy Apostles' experience parallels our own. We have plenty of food for the poor and homeless in Memphis. Providing more food is not the solution to homelessness. The issue is in the *heart*, not the stomach.

Most Homeless People Will Share What They Have with Others

We always thought people with money were the only ones to give. Not so. Generosity is alive and well in urban America. Last month, a homeless man named Mike visited our downtown church service. Someone on the street told him about the meal we share together after worship. During the service, Mike listened attentively to the sermon and took the Lord's Supper. When the offering plate came by, Mike hesitated. He had no money. Then he reached into his pocket. He put one of his last two bus tokens in the plate.

Such sharing occurs regularly. Eula often stays with her daughter Jasmine, but usually lives in an abandoned YMCA building downtown with several of her homeless friends. When Eula gets an occasional sack of vegetables from St. Patrick's, she doesn't hoard it, but shares her good fortune with others. Ironically, she often gives the staff of our inner-city ministry a good part of her vegetable wealth. Where's the irony in that? The poor see sharing as an expression of their wealth. They are eager to give, even when they have little.

One cold day, Ron and Anthony found three men sharing a fire barrel under a bridge. As they got closer, they saw that the men used the barrel to warm their hands and cook their food. They graciously offered the warmth of their fire and the meager meal they prepared in a tin pot. They asked nothing in return.

Stereotypical images of the poor often suggest hands begging for money. While inner-city people depend on such gifts to maintain life, many also understand the need to give to others. Many gifts directed at the poor are passed from one family to another.

Often one homeless person will make the homeless community aware of a church or agency that really wants to help. At a Blanket Giveaway involving a suburban church youth group and an inner-city church, Belinda, who spends most of her time on the streets, brought all her homeless friends to "share" in her good fortune. There is a godly sense of sharing among those who have little. Aid to the homeless often enters a distribution system of one homeless man sharing equally with another in a way we could never organize.

Some Homeless People Like Being Homeless

We don't want to be homeless. We don't even want to join Charles Landreth in his month-long trek on the streets. We can't imagine anybody wanting to be homeless. If we were suddenly homeless, we'd claw our way back to a "respectable" life.

We were shocked to learn that people like Norma are homeless by choice. She lived in an abandoned shotgun house. Glass from shattered windows littered the floor, discarded doors covered gaping holes in the rotted floor, and beer bottles filled the empty corners. One day, we dropped off an old mattress for Norma. She put it in the only room where the roof didn't leak. On other occasions, we helped Norma with food, clothing, and transportation. With time came trust.

When she finally asked us to help her find a more permanent place to live and a more stable source of income, we gladly agreed. Charlie, one of our ministers, set up a meeting with a social worker to talk with Norma about housing. Norma seemed uneasy. When she heard that housing was available, she began fidgeting. In the middle of the interview that promised to change her life and her housing situation, Norma stood up without a word and ran out of the room. Since that first encounter, we've repeated this process with Norma several times. Each time Norma bails out before finalizing arrangements. For reasons we cannot quite understand, Norma prefers her life on the streets to one in a house.

Working with Norma surprised us. Others may understand the Normas, Mikes, and Larrys who, despite our regular efforts to provide permanent housing, choose to live on the streets. We still have a relationship with them, and they still come to church. We're still willing to assist whenever they are ready to receive help. We're still struggling with how to bring the compassion of Christ to people caught in desperate situations.

Most Homeless People Are Frightened

Homeless people scare us. They seem fearless as they ask for money, but what we often miss is their fear. What could be more frightening than living on the streets of urban America?

What could be more frightening than living on the streets of urban America?

Churches in several American cities sponsor a "Room in the Inn" program which houses homeless people in church buildings during the cold months of the year. One or two nights a month, each congregation provides volunteers to meet the homeless people at the downtown registration center and transport them by bus to the church gymnasium or multipurpose room which is set up with cots. In Nashville, the Room in the Inn program uses a metal detector to screen all people seeking shelter. They started using the metal detector at the insistence of the homeless people. They wouldn't come to Room in the Inn unless they knew they would be safe.

Deanna was homeless. She and her three children started attending an inner-city church when fire swept through the abandoned house where she was living, forcing her out on the street. With no job and no money, she turned to a friend who loaned her a house in which to live. Anthony and Harold dropped by with four grocery bags filled with food and supplies. When they arrived at her new house on a beautiful spring afternoon, the door was shut and the window curtains drawn. Harold said, "Anthony, she's not home." They knocked, the door opened, and they went in. Deanna and her two-year-old son were watching the fuzzy picture on an old TV. She was happy to see them. They made some awkward small talk. Her little boy wanted to go outside, but she wouldn't let him.

It was then they saw her fear. She wouldn't let her son go outside because she was afraid. She kept the curtains drawn because she was afraid. Over each window, she had balanced one of the boy's little toys, a fire truck over one window, a plastic hammer on another. It was her security system. If somebody tried to break in, the rattling would shake the toy loose, it would fall to the floor, make a noise, and alert her to the intruder.

She had a board wedged into brackets to keep the door shut, like they did on *Little House on the Prairie*. She put the little boy's baby picture on the bar bracing the door. Any attempt to break in through the door would have pushed the picture onto the floor, shattering the glass.

Ron and Harold talked to a man at the Union Mission. One of the reasons he preferred spending the night there was because other homeless men would steal from him if he slept in the alleys around the midtown medical center. Confronting fear can be the critical obstacle in dealing with homelessness. Although we must overcome our fear of the homeless, in the long run, we must find ways to allow Jesus to calm the tremendous fear which many poor people face every waking and sleeping moment.

The World of the Homeless Is Small

Urban scholars talk about cognitive maps, which explain how we see the world. When we say "east," most suburbanites think of China or New England or the suburbs on the east side of the city. We have a global cognitive map. Most inner-city dwellers live in a smaller world. Cedric has lived in the Foote Homes area for eighteen years. As we talked with Cedric, we tried to reconstruct his cognitive map. His world includes the local office for food vouchers, two small neighborhood grocery stores, four churches which serve meals and give out bus tokens, two comfortable shelters, the city hospital, a clinic for the poor, and the Mental Health Center. Cedric doesn't think about the world beyond those dozen places.

Poplar Avenue bisects the city of Memphis with as many people living north of this broad boulevard as south. The Downtown Church is six blocks south of Poplar. Sharon lives in a rundown apartment with fifteen other people just off Poplar. Her entire world exists between the church and her apartment. The first time Anthony took her home, he asked her where she lived. She replied, "North Memphis." Anthony geared up for a long trip through the north part of the city. After six blocks, she said, "We're here." Obscured by her poverty and limited by her lack of education, Sharon's world is only a square mile in the middle of a major city.

Many Homeless People Have Psychiatric Problems

Most people we encounter in a day's routine behave normally. We relate to and love "normal" people more easily than folks who fall outside our accepted standards of behavior. Street people frequently exhibit behaviors that frighten or confuse us. One in three has a psychiatric illness.

At the church service one morning, Larry sat down beside Anthony. During the service, he walked around nervously, constantly watching the door. Finally, he shouted, "There are eleven cop cars out there looking for me, but I didn't do it." We looked outside. There were no police, just paranoia.

Keith's trademark is a red bandanna and tight pants. He works as a male prostitute. His uncle wants to care for him, but Keith's erratic lifestyle strains the relationship.

Once Mike, laughing uncontrollably, threatened to kill Anthony over a plate of food at an outreach dinner. Dissatisfied with the meal, Mike shattered the plate on the floor for emphasis as he made his threat. Men from the congregation escorted him out. Moments later, Anthony offered Mike another plate of food. Mike acted as if nothing had happened.

Training in counseling helps us to identify and serve such people. Any work among American homeless people will call for some kind of psychological expertise to serve in an advisory and training role.

These six insights about homeless people do not surprise seasoned workers among the poor, but they shocked us during our first years of helping the underclass. They revealed the amazing complexity of homelessness in America and showed us that providing help is more than mattresses and meals. As we increasingly understand the nature of homelessness, we can more readily see how the resources and talents of our churches can be used most effectively.

Until we know what it means to be homeless in America, we'll limit our efforts to reach them.

Charles Landreth took a risk walking the streets of downtown Dallas. We understand why he did it. Until we know what it means to be homeless in America, we'll limit our efforts to reach them. Serving the homeless means overcoming our own reservations before we enter their world.

---

1. Noah Snider, *When There's No Place Like Home: An Autobiography of the Homeless* (Nashville: Nelson, 1991), p. 229.

Chapter Three Action Plans

1. Take a group of two other people with you early Saturday morning and visit the local bar strip. Take a bag of fast food breakfast biscuits and hand them out to the homeless you see. Stop and talk with them.

2. Investigate what your community is doing to house the homeless and poor.

3. Get out a map of your city. Highlight the areas that are considered "poor" and "high crime" areas. Pray for them daily.

4. Read James 5:1-6 and discuss what it means to be rich and James's warnings.

5. Consider your church's food pantry. Are there opportunities for its recipients to "connect" with its workers?

Apprentice Chris Stewart brings AIDS sufferer Taya to Anthony Wood's home after hospice care.

Norma tells us of the difficulties of being homeless as we bring her a mattress to sleep on in
the abandoned building where she lives.

Eunice, who started her street business
at 14 years old, came to The
Downtown Church for help and prayer.

Downtown Church member Sharon shares a Thanksgiving turkey, provided by area churches, with Stella.

Teens volunteer at Power Hour to teach
inner city children about God in the projects.

CHAPTER 4

A Whole New Brotherhood!

"If a free society cannot help the many who are poor, it cannot save the few who are rich."

—John F. Kennedy

The glass door to the old grocery store leads us into a large room with a high ceiling. The folding chairs set in a semicircle are all full. Quite a crew has gathered. The lady in the pink dress has AIDS. The two teenage boys on the back row were released from juvenile detention this past week. The two women in short skirts used to be prostitutes. The man with the red T-shirt served fifteen years for murder. The man next to him spent nearly a decade in prison for arson. The family that fills the third row is finally back together again. The parents have been separated four times in the last two years.

Who are these people? A meeting of the local AA? A support group for troubled families? Members of a neighborhood watch association? A group gathered to advocate for a new parole system? No, none of the above.

It's a church! People drawn out of prison and off the streets by Jesus. Women who have given up drugs and men who have put aside crime for the sake of Christ. When they sing, "You oughta been there when He saved my soul,"[1] they remember how it was. When they sing, "The things I used to do, I don't do them anymore,"[2] they remember exactly who taught them differently. They understand something about how broken a body can be, which gives them a deep appreciation for the Body broken for them.

We didn't expect that at the beginning. We thought we could put all the inner-city people and all the suburbanites into one big church. After all, it looks like a perfect match. A person without hope meets people with hope. A person needing acceptance and affirmation encounters a group with acceptance and affirmation to spare. The one is down, the other is looking for somebody to lift up. Did we have a match?

No.

People from the suburbs who work among urban poor are the matchmakers. To us, the marriage looked made in heaven. They needed help. We wanted to help. Insert key into door and unlock.

A Room in the City Can Become a Cell in Jail

Wrong key? Wrong door? Where did we go wrong? Latisha is a case in point. Reared in the Mississippi Delta in a shotgun house, raised on welfare checks, Latisha reached adulthood with one conclusion: *"It has to be better somewhere else."*

Latisha moved to the city looking for a way out of poverty, but found her way into jail. With no job skills, no money, no contacts, she found herself working the corner of Vance and Lauderdale, selling the only thing she had left: her body. Her boarding house doubled as a crack house. "Drive through" traffic offered all kinds of business opportunities. She hated it. Hated her roach-infested home. Hated the "dates." Hated the pimps. Hated the cocaine that numbed her mind as it drove her deeper into poverty. The city became a prison, her pimp became her warden, the bad landlords and drug dealers the prison guards. Life is hard in Memphis's inner city. But you get used to anything when you've got nowhere to go.

It was an average night for business at Vance and Lauderdale in the summer of 1993. With his Friday paycheck cashed and booze on his breath, a man approached Latisha on the corner. Before they discussed price, sirens and flashing blue lights filled the intersection. Booked for solicitation. "Always at the wrong place at the wrong time," Latisha thought as she gritted her teeth. From courthouse to prison, Latisha cursed her fate, the judge, the system, and her own life. Filled with hatred for everything and everybody, Latisha became the newest resident in Shelby County Correctional Center.

Inside the green prison walls, drugs were plentiful, the food good, the company tolerable. Shotgun shack to unknown man's bed to prison – life had been a sorry journey. One day she noticed she looked like her cellmates. Same talk. Same walk. Same orange jumpsuit. "When did that happen?" she wondered. Yet there was a difference. They seemed tough, confident, defiant. She felt weak, uncertain, compliant. She decided to become a steel mask, impenetrable to all. Steel. That's what she wanted to be. Hard as a gun barrel and twice as threatening. Determined to harden her heart, she became like them. It was the only way to survive. Then the unexpected happened.

God Introduces Us to a New Family

Don Matthews came to the prison chapel one Sunday night. Latisha didn't go to worship, she just wanted out of the cell for an hour. At least, that's what the steel mask made her say. She sat in the back of the large room. Other prisoners filed in, some to sing praises, others to do a little "business" despite the guard's careful eye. The prayers were thoughtful, the singing reminded her of "down home." Then Don, the speaker for the night, talked about Jesus. Latisha thought, "Yeah, right. Where's Jesus now?"

She smiled as she remembered her auntie taking her to church twenty-two years ago. "Old folks religion," the steel chided within her. "Ain't no Jesus gonna love a slut like you." Could Jesus love her? The steel tried to repress the question, but Latisha fought back.

Latisha went to the Tuesday night Bible study Don offered, thinking, "Maybe I'll at least get cigarette money out of this guy." She knew how to do it, leaning over, unzipping her bright orange prison suit just enough for him to take a peek. He didn't look. He kept talking about Jesus, uninterested in her flirtations.

Slowly God's unconditional love penetrated the steel barrier around her heart. Don assured her, "There's nothing you've done too long or too bad that Jesus can't forgive." In time she let Jesus inside the steel barricade. Her life changed. Her friendship with Don grew. The feelings of hopelessness shrank.

"There's nothing you've done too long or too bad that Jesus can't forgive."

A new family waited for her on the outside. Don's description of a wonderful church eagerly waiting to meet her was hard to believe. Latisha fought the nervousness. She wondered if it was true.

The judge reduced Latisha's charge. With good behavior and a work release program, Latisha was out in eight months. Her heart swelled at the thought of finally meeting her new church family. She'd never felt so happy. No more escaping. Finally she had direction in her life.

Don asked *her* to ride to church with his family. She was amazed at their love and concern. Don introduced her to everyone. They all seemed so nice. Latisha didn't think about it until later, but she had left her steel mask in her prison cell, along with her past. Her first day at church was like heaven itself. They sang, prayed, studied the Bible. During the communion service, she silently prayed, "Thank you, Lord, for my new home!" This new church was going to be everything she dreamed.

Sometimes We Feel as though We Don't Fit

After the newness of the first week at church, things changed. Something didn't feel right. Even though Don made her feel welcome, even though all the others smiled, she felt out of place. This was not what she'd hoped for, not what she'd been told it would be like.

Latisha wasn't dressed in the latest fashion, but the outfit she had picked from the clothes closet was respectable. Her hair wasn't the newest style, but it was neat and clean. After all, Don had told her, "Jesus takes you just the way you are." Makeup wasn't in the budget just yet, but Don said it was the heart that mattered. Her grammar was often incorrect, but she was completing her GED.

The songs weren't those she had sung as a child or in the Sunday worship at the Correctional Center. Everything seemed so stiff, formal, and lifeless. These were good people, but so unlike her. Suddenly panic set in, right in the pew. The old feelings chilled her heart. A steel mask descended as an inner voice whispered, "I told you. You don't belong here. You belong to me." Suddenly she wanted to escape. But where? Back home? The streets? The boarding house? She attended church services for several weeks, but slowly drifted back to a past she thought she had escaped. Back to the streets.

We usually don't see the story from Latisha's point of view. The poor come for a couple of weeks and disappear. We rationalize. Some seed sprouts immediately only to die quickly. The cares of the world get another one. But for Latisha, the seed of God didn't die. No worldly weeds blocked the sunlight. She just didn't fit.

We had trouble understanding her feeling until we experienced it ourselves. Anthony knows something of her discomfort.

Jesus Overcomes Cultural Differences

I [Anthony] don't fit in the inner city. I'm white. I'm a somewhat rural redneck with a little education from south Mississippi in the projects. I'm middle class in the midst of the underclass. Early in our work, on Sunday morning, I looked around the inner-city congregation, and I felt out of place. I didn't seem to fit. People were friendly and warm, but the songs were not the songs I remembered, the tenor of the service was not the same as the one in the suburbs. I began to understand how Latisha felt. I was different.

I've stayed because I learned that Jesus overcomes those differences. Jesus preached to the Samaritans, touched lepers, ate with tax collectors and consorted with prostitutes. Jesus brings everyone together.

Jesus brings everyone together.

My parents modeled that message of compassion and acceptance. Dad preached for a local black church across town when they were between ministers. Once he brought a recently paroled ex-offender home for supper. My mother cleaned house for an elderly black lady named Rosie who lived "across the tracks." I witnessed a gospel that closed gaps between people.

I also understand how Don felt. Don sensed Latisha's discomfort. He saw fellow Christians hesitate when Latisha sat down with them at a fellowship dinner. He noticed she didn't know the songs. He heard the preacher use words she didn't understand. He knew the formal service seemed foreign to her. She began to miss church. Angry and hurt, he began to question the gospel call for unity. Where was God's family? Where was the support for the weak and the poor preached from the pulpit? Where was the accepting of those "not like me" talked about last week in Bible class? Where was the building of relationships with the lowly, the outcast? Those words rang hollow and empty in his ears when Latisha went back to the streets.

Don took his concerns to one of the elders who had been a missionary in Africa for ten years. Knowing that Ken loved the lost, Don talked about Latisha's struggle to blend in with the church, about his own frustration with church members who seemed aloof. Don's eyes teared and his throat tightened as he shared Latisha's uncertain feelings after attending church that first week out of jail. Don finished by asking, "What should we do now?"

There was a long silence. Ken shook his head slowly, knowing he could not provide the answer Don needed. "Our church is not ready to minister to people like Latisha." Latisha, Don, and Ken all came to the same conclusion: not everyone fits into God's church.

We know the feeling. We want the poor, the ex-offender, the homeless to feel welcome at our churches, but no matter how hard we try, how much we care, they don't. They find few real relationships, little meaningful fellowship, no feeling of belonging. It's just another place from which to escape after their emergency needs have been met. We have our clothing rooms, our Thanksgiving dinner giveaways, our special Christmas time projects, but they all miss the mark. Good motives undergird our efforts because we want them to know a loving Jesus and his church. Yet the poor walk away with the greatest need still heavy on their hearts.

What's the solution? Where do we go wrong? Why does the "perfect match" so often go awry? We found the answers not in the projects, but in the Gospels.

God Knows the Needs of the Poor

John 1:14 says Jesus came "to dwell among us." He did not call us to join him in heaven. He came to us. He adapted to our world, not we to his. He took our form, our life, our culture, came to our neighborhood, breathed our air, walked our streets. He met us on our own ground. Jesus left his comfort zone, became vulnerable, open to hunger, fatigue, disappointment, and pain. He gave up his fellowship with the Father, the Holy Spirit, and the angels to join ours.

We welcome the poor into our middle-class churches with open arms. Yet in that gracious act, we still expect them to adapt to our culture, our church, our worship style. But Jesus took a different approach. Like him, we must meet the Latishas in their own world. We must follow Jesus all the way in our openness.

Just as we found Jesus in our world, the poor deserve to find Jesus in their world.

Just as we found Jesus in our world, the poor deserve to find Jesus in their world. God doesn't have a suburban address. The poor can find God in their own neighborhood. God has been in the inner city long before we ever arrived. Just as others have started Hispanic churches to reach Hispanics, and Korean churches to reach Koreans, we must plant inner-city churches for the inner-city poor.

It is not necessary to become a suburbanite to follow Jesus in America. God knows the needs of the poor because he was from among them and lived with them. The poor will be drawn to and stay in churches that they can call their own. The poor may not attend middle-class congregations, but they will embrace God's church.

Part of the hesitancy of the poor to stay in suburban churches comes from our minimizing of cultural differences. Just because we speak the same language does not mean that we can communicate with each other. The inner-city person lives in as different a world from ours as that of a Rwandan refugee's. Dr. Evertt Huffard, who often speaks about urban ministry, says, "It was easier for a rural Tennessean to go to Africa in 1950 to do mission work than it is for a suburbanite to go to the American inner city in 1995." We would add, "This is still true in 2000!" Cultural differences between the inner city and the suburbs are immense. The same differences exist between the inner-city churches and the suburban congregations.

There is growing interest in planting churches which reflect the culture of the inner city, center on the spiritual needs of the poor, and deal in a holistic way with the complexities of urban America. Church plantings in major metropolitan areas show positive results. Some have large numbers attending. The poor will come — and stay — when we bring the gospel to their culture like Jesus brought it to ours.

Understanding Brings the Gospel to the Poor

We learned three things in starting inner-city churches. *First, respect inner-city culture.* Effective missionaries study the culture first. We mistakenly believe inner-city dwellers are either just like us or inferior to us. Neither is true. Each urban center has its own culture, values, and language that must be learned through study and observation.

Insensitivity to different cultures creates *barriers* instead of bridges.

Insensitivity to different cultures creates *barriers* instead of bridges. Missionaries learned to bring Christ, not their hometown culture, to a new country. Jesus loved people by respecting them. We will do the same. Here are a few ways to get started:

1) Educate your church biblically, culturally, and missiologically concerning urban church planting and ministry. Read books like Ray Bakke's *The Urban Christian* or William Pannell's *The Gospel from the Bottom Up*.

2) Visit an existing inner-city church that is reaching the urban poor to appreciate the faith practiced in cultural diversity. Research what others have done.

3) Ask people knowledgeable about the local poor to guide you through the existing outreach programs in your city.

4) Ask a poor person for honest answers about why he doesn't attend church where you do. Brace yourself for the truth. Then ask your new friend, "If there was a church in your neighborhood that you would go to every week, what would it be like?"

Second, expect inner-city leadership. We found more sense of community in the poorer areas of town than we've ever experienced in the affluent sections. The inner-city neighborhood has a social structure and leadership network. There is a saying in our inner city, "It takes a whole community to raise a child." Family, school, social service, and church all connect. Networks flourish in the inner city. Church workers can connect to these networks. Our goal is to establish a fellowship of inner-city churches with local leadership designed to serve their own communities. The church must be built according to this urban blueprint. Our inner-city brothers and sisters are better equipped to take back their neighborhoods for Christ by using their own networks to build God's church community.

Third, expect inner-city theologians to arise. The Bible established doctrine, but Christians develop traditions. We establish the order of a Sunday morning service, decide how long the sermon should be, work out details on who can spend church money. Suburban preachers speak to issues that confront the average middle-class American. While fundamental doctrines do not vary, their application and meaning varies, depending on the situation of the local Christians.

In our suburban church, ushers stand at the back of the auditorium to serve. If a homeless woman tried to walk to the front during the sermon, they would stop her and talk with her in the foyer. To suburbanites, that seems a reasonable and loving policy. To inner-city Christians, that policy is offensive and unacceptable. They know that people often come into the service as a last resort. To turn away a homeless woman at that critical time may lead her to drugs or to her seeking help from different people. They value an uninterrupted sermon just like the people in the suburbs, but they understand the rejection of forcing a homeless person to wait.

Inner-city people, when exposed regularly to the unchanging teaching of God's will, begin to see how it plays out in their own setting. Only when the gospel is communicated in terms understood in the urban setting will it become a fire that cannot be extinguished.

Why don't they come to our church? There's one good reason — too many congregations reflect our culture, not theirs. When people like Latisha fall away, it may not be lack of faith. It may just be a sense of being out of place. Memphis Urban Ministry plants churches where the Latishas can find their places.

There's hope for all the Latishas in churches that reflect their culture, that understand their plight, that are patient with differing lifestyles, that are willing to cross cultural barriers.

"Workcamp" is a simple idea. Christian teenagers paint houses of poor elderly people in the inner city. They pay a small fee to cover the paint costs. Local restaurants donate food. Christian families loan their ladders. Recently some 450 teenagers and adults from 23 churches painted 31 houses in four days. After the last day of painting, the homeowners and the teen-aged workers gathered for a banquet to celebrate the completion of the work and the newfound friendships.

During the banquet, one of the speakers mentioned that one of the youth groups participating in Workcamp was quite special. They were from the Downtown Church. They were part of the army of teens that slapped 575 gallons of paint on thirsty Memphis houses. When their name was mentioned, the teens from the Downtown Church jumped to their feet and cheered. It was a milestone for them. Living in poverty, surrounded by violence, walking streets with substandard housing, they had now achieved something they never dreamed possible – they were a church. They were a church that reflected their culture and their understanding. Just as our congregations give us a spiritual identity and provide us a spiritual home, now these teens had found the same thing.

We dreamed of a day when we in Memphis would not have just one inner-city sister congregation, but we prayed for a day when there would be an entire brotherhood of such churches, places where the Latishas of life can find not only God, but a home. God has given us five new churches.

---

1. "Said I Wasn't," author unknown.
2. "The Things I Used to Do," author unknown.

Chapter Four Action Plans

1. Read Harlon Dalton's *Racial Healing: Confronting the Fear between Blacks and Whites.* New York: Anchor Books, 1985.

2. Open a dialogue about race with an African-American, a Hispanic, or an Oriental friend.

3. Attend an African-American church service or a Hispanic congregation (in English).

4. Start a Bible class in your church to discuss racism and prejudice.

5. Discuss the three suggestions made at the close of this chapter.

CHAPTER 5

The Multicolored Jesus

We have run away from race far too long. We are so afraid
of inflaming the wound that we fail to deal with what remains
America's central social problem.

—Harlan L. Dalton[1]

Signs Are Meant to Be Read

There it was. Clear as day. Three lines. The top line blared out the
news in the oldest of the three scripts. It was the language used by
Moses, Samuel, David, and Solomon — Hebrew, the language of the
Ten Commandments, the script of the prophet Isaiah, the holy tongue
of the synagogue.

Most Americans would have only recognized the script from the
middle line. It used the same letters as English, but the words were clear
only to those who knew it. Although the tongue had been used by the
ancient Latium, it was the Romans who made Latin a world language,
one that would dominate the human civilization for the next thousand
years. It was the middle line, because the Romans erected the sign. The
Hebrew line informed the locals; the middle line made it official.

Most who passed by the sign would have recognized either the
top line or the middle one, but not both. Everybody could read the

bottom inscription in Greek — the world language. From housewives writing their shopping lists to young lovers expressing intimate thoughts, the world knew Greek.

All three lines — Hebrew, Latin, and Greek — said the same thing, each line speaking to a different culture. Each reflected the alienation of one people from another. Each stood for a way of thinking that the others could often not understand. The same sign, lettered in three different languages, because racial and cultural divisions have plagued humanity since the days after the Flood.

Translated into a fourth language, the three lines said, "Jesus of Nazareth, the King of the Jews."

The sign hung over the cross.

Although the sign makers simply meant to identify the man on the middle cross, they indirectly conveyed a theological message. The man under the sign transcended culture. He wasn't only for the Hebrews. Nor did he come just for the mighty Romans. Jesus didn't appeal only to the philosophical Greeks. In a way, the three lines indicated that Jesus is for everybody. There was no line in German or English, Sanskrit or Creole, but what happened at the cross went far beyond Jew, Roman, or Greek.

The World Refuses to Learn from the Cross

Ironically, humanity refuses to learn the lesson of the sign over the cross. People who speak different languages and practice different customs perpetuate mutual hatred in Ireland, the former Yugoslavia, South Africa, and dozens of other spots around the world. The American city is no exception. Prejudice against African Americans, Hispanics, Asians, Native Americans, and other groups continues unabated. Anybody who works among the unchurched in America will quickly hear one central objection to Christianity: "The most segregated time during the week is Sunday morning." Schools, businesses, government offices, military forces, and a host of other institutions are integrated, but most American churches meet in segregated units.

"The most segregated time during the week is Sunday morning."

The sign above the cross has tremendous implications for work among the poor. Just as the cross transcended the cultural, racial, and social differences of that day, those who serve the disenfranchised must navigate the same gaps today. Even if the poor speak the same language and belong to the same race, the social and economic differences still create a set of barriers to overcome.

The task of facing the racial and economic gaps in our city intimidates and bothers us. We find hope in Jesus who said, "If I be lifted up, I will draw *all* men unto myself." That's what the sign said: Hebrews, Latins, Greeks. All are invited. All are expected. All are welcome. The sign over the cross didn't define his appeal to all; the One on the cross did. We've found the cross a valuable guide as we've reflected on our own past, as we have pondered our current relationships, and as we seek for Christian reconciliation in an alienated world.

A second cross is not in Jerusalem, but in Memphis. It's not on a hillside, but inside a remodeled grocery store now called the Downtown Church. It's made of wood, but also of acrylic paint on rough cement blocks. It's not Roman, it's American. Ours is a reflection of the original. Twenty feet high, it towers over the room that used to market greens and tomatoes, but now heralds the message of grace and truth.

But the Memphis cross differs from the Jerusalem cross in one other significant way. The modern artist used color to bring out one of the central points of the cross. The Jesus painted by the artist is multicolored. Not a white Jesus. Not a black Jesus. Not a red Jesus. Not a yellow Jesus. But a Jesus of all colors.

The Memphis inner city is ninety-nine percent black. The picture on the wall immediately communicates. They know what the colors mean. They understand the message of the one who died. The multicolored Jesus speaks clearly.

It hasn't been easy getting to the multicolors. The Jesus on the wall brings all the colors together. Much of Anthony's past was spent keeping the colors apart.

Racism Is Learned at an Early Age

I [Anthony] grew up in a racist culture. My grandpa served as Deputy Sheriff of Bolivar County, Mississippi, and later as Patrolman for the Clarksdale, Mississippi, Police Department during the fifties and sixties. He died when I was two years old. My basic memory of Grandpa centers on a dresser drawer full of guns, knives, billy clubs, and other weapons taken from criminals. After his death, Grandma would fascinate me by allowing a peek into that drawer. Once I found an oddly misshapen bullet. Grandma explained, "Oh, that's the bullet from the only man your Grandpa ever shot." Noticing the look of surprise on my face, she hurriedly added, "But he shot him in the leg." Struggling to satisfy a young boy's puzzlement, Grandma said, "Oh, don't worry, he was only a 'n—r.'"

Carol Ann sat behind me in fourth grade geography class at Washington Elementary in my hometown of Natchez, Mississippi. It was 1968. The whole class was white except for Carol Ann. I didn't mind sitting near Carol Ann, but didn't say much to her. One hot Tuesday afternoon, Carol Ann threw up on the floor beside her desk. Even though she was obviously sick, the teacher made Carol Ann get the mop from the janitor and clean up the mess herself. I made a move to help a little, wanted to do more, but didn't. The other kids held their noses saying, "Yuck, 'n—r' puke." The smell didn't bother me as much as my pain for Carol Ann, who was the object of such ridicule because of her race. I felt shame for not helping her more.

In fifth grade, Orlando and I played cowboys and Indians at recess and ate together at lunch. There were no other black boys at Washington Elementary. One day, a gang of white boys beat up my black playmate. In disbelief, I heard the playground teacher blame it on Orlando. I knew better, but said nothing. I watched it happen, but did nothing. Orlando and I didn't seem to be as close after that.

I sat behind Cindy Minor in eleventh grade English. I kept our conversations to a minimum, unless no one else was in the room. As we talked before class one day, she offered me half of her Snickers™ bar. As I silently reached out to break off a piece, someone walked into the room and groaned, "Ugh." Then I heard the whisper, "You're gonna take that from her?"

With my hand suspended in midair, I weighed Gene's comment. Should I eat a piece of candy touched by a black person or offend Cindy? My fingers never touched the chocolate. Cindy mumbled something like, "I see." Those two words were the last we ever exchanged.

I called blacks "n—rs." I roughhoused with black guys as we ran track, but ignored them in the mall. I saw blacks do well in class, but on the street joked about how all blacks were lazy. I dated a girl whose father was an active member of the Ku Klux Klan. I remember the crosses burning on the highway south of town.

The culture screamed for segregation.
The cross called for reconciliation.

The racist culture demanded: "Hate blacks!" The cross demanded: "End hatred!" The culture screamed for segregation. The cross called for reconciliation. My culture dislikes those who are different. The cross sets a higher standard of liking all, regardless of differences.

A Proper Understanding of the Cross Eliminates Racism

Several significant events in my life helped me to understand that multicolored cross. One was living among people who had overcome racism. After graduating from high school in Mississippi, I lived in Alaska for two years. The church I attended had a black elder and a black deacon with a white wife. Some of the single white men shared apartments with single black men. The same was true for some of the single girls. The togetherness shocked me at first, but then I saw how people led by the cross could overcome the divisions of race.

A second event in Mississippi stood in contrast to my Alaska experience, but has propelled my own desire to seek a multicolored Jesus. While in Alaska I met my wife, Candi. After our marriage, Candi got her first dose of bigotry in a most unexpected place one Wednesday night. Arriving late for Bible class one cool March evening, we hurried into the worship service at a local church. We were greeted warmly by a brother at the door.

A few moments later, a black couple arrived. We overheard them apologize for arriving late, but express their joy at finding a church. The same brother smiled and said, "There's a church across town where you would feel more comfortable." Their faces fell. They weren't welcome.

That night, the Bible class studied the Great Commission. When the teacher, the same brother, got to the part about preaching the gospel to "every creature," he affirmed that we shouldn't be selective about the people we share the gospel with. The teacher smiled, looked directly at me and my wife, and explained, "And blacks are creatures, too." Their inconsistency between theology and practice reminded me of my own racist past and hardened my own commitment to see that multicolored Jesus.

As I've come to understand the cross, I've become more aware of my own guilt with regard to racism and my own need to reconcile. The cross has freed me from my past. I no longer choose friends or work based on race. With Paul I say, "We look at people no longer from a worldly point of view" (2 Cor 5:16).

The inner-city church I work with is less than a mile from the National Civil Rights Museum. I visit and financially support this institution which marks the spot in Memphis where Dr. Martin Luther King, Jr. was shot. In the museum, a row of Plexiglas™ cases displays racial atrocities recorded by the NAACP during the fifties and sixties.

Many of those incidents happened in Bolivar County and Clarksdale, Mississippi, at the time Grandpa served on the force. I wonder, "Did Grandpa participate?"

As I have come to face my past, I have felt a strong need to apologize, to seek forgiveness for what I did. I'm sorry about my heritage. As one who has benefited from a racist and segregated society socially and economically, I feel an apology on my part is legitimate. I apologize regularly to the African Americans that I meet. Many are now my friends. Although God at the cross has forgiven me of my sins, the cross raises another significant issue not just for me, but for all of us.

We know the problems of our society: racism, wretched housing, class division, stereotyping, gender bias, ethnic prejudice, an unjust economic system. Our cities overflow with subcultures at odds with each other. Neighborhoods split with other neighborhoods over irreconcilable differences. One group oppresses another. Who is responsible for fixing these problems? Who should take the leadership role in bringing people together? Forgiveness is a cross-centered matter. That makes it church business.

Forgiveness is a cross-centered matter.

The church must be a catalyst in bridging the gaps between segments of our society. Where is forgiveness needed more than in our cities? Before there can be reconciliation, there must be dialogue. Before there is dialogue, there must be an apology. Before there is an apology, there must be a willingness to forgive and seek forgiveness. Before there can be a willingness to forgive and seek forgiveness, there must be a people living in the shadow of the cross.

We cannot cover a hidden agenda of bigotry with a layer of separate but equal churches.

While we recognize the cultural differences between the inner city and suburban America, we cannot accept any form of racism. We cannot cover a hidden agenda of bigotry with a layer of separate but equal churches. Racism is wrong. It is sin.

In our first years of working among the poor, we agonized over the issue of race and poverty. As we repeatedly invited the poor blacks into our white churches, we wondered how to serve and nurture them to faithfulness. Yet our middle-class congregations proved ineffective at nurturing the poor of any race. By establishing a congregation to meet the spiritual needs of the poor, the poor have come to Christ. And we've seen the power of the multicolored Jesus.

We're an odd pair walking across the courtyard at Cleaborn Homes. One underclass. One middle class. One black. One white. Junior and I minister together. He was the first black man I met in the projects. Once in two different worlds, we now live in the shadow of the same cross. We study and pray together. We share our lunches in town and a hotel room when we're out of town. Together we planted a church in the middle of the projects.

After two years of ministering together and to each other, Junior started one of our heart-to-heart talks by reporting on a shooting. He noted that when the bystanders call for help, the first question they are asked is, "Who is it?" In this case they answered, "A black male." Then Junior unpacked one of the realities of the inner city. If the victim is black, it may be three hours before police arrive to investigate. Then Junior smiled, "But Anthony, if you get shot, they'll have the helicopters out in twenty minutes looking for who did it."

What could I say? We, a black and a white, were friends in a racist society. I said that it was wrong, unjust, racist, and I apologized. Then Junior's face went from smile to peacefulness as he said, "But you know, Anthony, I no longer see you as a white man, but just as a man." Junior pointed to his Bible, "It's only because of this, man."

The cross brings oneness in a world of racial hate.

As Cleaborn Homes resident Gloria gave her life to Christ, she expressed the joy of having a new church family that was both black and white. The multicolored Jesus made a difference for her. Years ago a white mob killed her grandfather. He hit a white man who used a racial slur against him.

After about three months of attending our children's outreach, little Kiki pulled on my shirt. As I bent down, she reached up with a wonderful hug.

"I like you, Mr. Anthony."

I replied, "I like you too, Kiki. In fact, I love you."

Her puzzled face reflected the cultural tension, "And you're white."

After Ladies Workday, Debra pulled Candi to the side and told her that she needed to cut her hair because she was starting to look like a "white woman." Candi smiled, "I am a white woman." They both laughed.

The man on the cross doesn't look at skin color.

Five of us attended the graduation of a young assistant minister. Mrs. Bea, an African American church member, went with Candi and me, along with Jeff and Veronica, the black brother and his wife who now minister to the Downtown Church. After the ceremony, Mrs. Bea's sister asked her about the event. She asked if any other black people were there. Mrs. Bea thought a moment, "Sure! There was Jeff and Veronica, Candi and Anthony . . . ."

We've come a long way, thanks to the multicolored man on the Cross. You'll read it on the front of T-shirts that say "Our God Don't See No Color!" You'll hear it in testimony time on Sunday, "God accepts black, white, yellow, green, and everything in between."

Three Suggestions That Will Promote Racial Harmony

1. Develop interracial friendships. Communication and understanding enhance strong relationships. All of us have sought friendships across racial lines. Important to this kind of friendship is exchanging hospitality. Until people eat together, acceptance is limited. Some of our closest friendships with the poor blacks in the inner city occur over our kitchen table. We eat together, invite their kids to spend the night, host Easter egg hunts in our back yard, and have them in for movie nights. When our homes are their homes, the wall of the white suburban, middle class barrier slowly breaks down. They realize they are welcome in our world. They have already welcomed us in theirs.

Until people eat together, acceptance is limited.

The depth of friendship varies. Even casual relationships enhance race relations. Black women in the projects watch over the white men and women who minister there. Jackie may invite us for an early dinner before Wednesday Prayer Meeting. Ms. Bobbie always offers a cold glass of lemonade for a minister on a hot August afternoon. Mrs. Bea always invites us in to enjoy the air conditioning when the temperature is in the nineties.

2. *Purposely pursue racially diverse leadership.* "Pepper and salt" turns up in all the planning documents of Memphis Urban Ministry, which emphasize shared black and white leadership. Not white at the top, but equal leadership, and in time, black at the top, since the neighborhood is ninety-nine percent black. When Jeff and Anthony walk in the neighborhood together, the message is clear that God put them together.

Developing racially diverse leadership calls for dedication. One Chicago church talks about the "principle of sacrifice in order to achieve reconciliation." When they appointed additional leaders in the congregation which is seventy percent black and thirty percent white, they decided it would be wrong to have seventy percent white elders and thirty percent black elders. Based on the "principle of sacrifice," some qualified white men were passed over.[2]

3. *Plan times for separated communities to be together.* We're associated with two large churches, one a predominantly white church of 1,600 members and the other a largely black congregation of 400. Twice a year, the two churches hold joint services under the theme,

"The Race Is One at the Cross." The services provide time for the two memberships to discuss and experience racial harmony.

David Galloway tells how one church sponsored a series of public forums on race in segregated Tyler, Texas. They sought to raise issues that the community would not face — issues about seeking and giving forgiveness.[2] When a tragedy fueled racial tensions, the community saw no violence. Galloway argues that the opening of dialogue and the discussion of forgiveness forged a new community response to an unfortunate racial event.

Those who stood around the cross saw the inscription in three different languages. But those who understood, and understand, what happened there know the deeper message. There can be harmony in the city.

---

1. Harlan L. Dalton, *Racial Healing* (New York: Anchor, 1995), p. 4.

2. Glen Kehrein, Henry Kwan, Russell Rosser, and Raleigh Washington, "From Many Nations, One Church," *Leadership* (Winter 1995): 125.

3. David A. Galloway, "Pastoring Your Community," *Leadership* (Summer 1995): 117-118.

Chapter Five Action Plans

1. Visit the homeless in prison.

2. Find out what prison ministries are active in your community. Talk with the chaplain at the local jail.

3. Make specific plans for implementing the three suggested activities at the end of the chapter.

4. Invite a missionary to talk with a small group about different styles of worship in the mission field. Discuss how you feel about allowing other cultures in your community to develop their own worship style.

Homeless men are welcomed to an Outreach meal
at The Downtown Church.

The Downtown Church gathers after Father's Day celebration.

The Downtown Church gathers in the shadow of the multicolored Jesus
believing "Our God don't see no color."

Downtown Church members and Highland St. Church youth
team up to share blankets with the Memphis homeless.

CHAPTER 6

Bare Cupboards and Empty Souls

The most important reason for evangelism is God's astounding, overflowing love for a lost and broken world.
—Ron Sider[1]

In *One-Sided Christianity*, Ron Sider makes an amazing observation about the work Christians do. Some Christians focus entirely on helping the poor. They set up shelters, organize job training programs, try to change structures to improve the lot of society's unfortunate. Others center only on spiritual issues. They see the cities teeming with lost people. They minister to the soul, set up Bible classes, organize prayer groups, and schedule preaching services. Sider concludes that while some help the poor and others evangelize among the lost, most Christians do neither. What perplexes Sider the most, however, is not that most Christians help *neither* the poor nor the lost, but that few are able to deal with *both* the poor and the lost. Few ministries set up shelters and seek out the soul. Not many of us are good at paying the light bill while raising the issue of the Light. The poor and the lost often remain in two separate categories.

While we struggle to evangelize among the poor, we feel the tension of combining service to the poor with a concern for their souls. It happened to Harold one Sunday after church.

Visitors Challenge Our Theology

The man was obviously a visitor. His T-shirt with the Coors™ Brewing Company logo was not the only thing that made him stand out in our largely middle class congregation. We were mostly a white church, he was black. We had cars, he was on foot. We were leaving, he just arrived. After greeting somebody in the parking lot, he asked if he could see the pastor. That's when he came to see me [Harold].

Without any introduction, he immediately poured out his story. He had a job, but was behind on the electric bill. The threat of being cut off the next day motivated his search for help. Each time he stopped at the church office during the week, he found the doors locked, so he came to services.

I stuck out my hand to introduce myself. I wanted to meet his physical need, but I also wondered how to offer something spiritual. He said he needed money, but what did his spirit need? His request was clearly about physical lack of light, not spiritual darkness.

He wasn't interested in bait and switch. He didn't want to sit through the sermon so he could sip soup. His request was physical, not spiritual. He came seeking the one and not the other. The tension between what he wanted to receive and what I wanted to give constricted me so that I barely knew how to respond. My hands, filled with the pressure of the day and shackled by my spiritual dilemma, left no room for a positive encounter. I didn't know what to do.

I explained the process we used at our congregation for helping people with utility bills. The potential of funds to pay off the light company may have thrilled his heart. The possibility that all he would get from us was a meager $43.26 for his arrears with Memphis Light, Gas, and Water burdened my soul.

I knew in my heart that I had not closed the distance between his world and mine. He had come to my world, but I had not moved into his. I felt that I had not conveyed to him any of the love of God that was in my heart, but had told him only about the funds our church had in the bank. I'd treated him in a kind, business-like manner, but we had not connected. We touched physically when we shook hands, but I didn't know what he really needed.

It all happened so fast. All those thoughts raced through my mind during our two-minute conversation. Desperately seeking some way to convey more than just a procedure for paying off the light company, I offered to have someone call him. I asked if he had a phone. As he wrote down the number, I promised somebody would call him that afternoon.

Then our eyes met. I have no idea what bounced around in his mind, but I felt that, in committing myself to seeking him out, perhaps I had offered more than temporary relief. He came begging. I honored him by offering to call. He arrived empty-handed. I treated his request with dignity. He came to my place. The next meeting would be at his place. He made all the effort. Now we would return the favor.

When I promised we would call, he smiled. Maybe because he heard the money jingling in his pocket. Maybe because he felt a concern for something beyond what he had asked. As I watched him walk away, I wondered how the story would end. Would we minister to his soul or merely satisfy his need?

Is it godly to offer spiritual assistance without addressing physical needs?

Encounters like the one Harold had at the church door raise probing questions. Is it helpful to serve a person physically without helping spiritually? Is it godly to offer spiritual assistance without addressing physical needs? If we pay off his electric bill, help him move to better housing, find him a better job, improve society so he has the opportunity for a better life, but never address his spiritual lostness, have we shown compassion in the eyes of God? If we teach him about Jesus, help him repent, lead him to salvation, train him in the spiritual disciplines of prayer, study, and church attendance, but leave him without food, in poor housing, without work, and in an unfair environment, have we helped that man in the eyes of God? Are there any circumstances where we can evangelize, but not be benevolent? Under what conditions do we show mercy but omit the message of the cross? Why do we feel tension when we pay the rent, but never address the soul? Why do we feel so guilty after knocking on the doors of inner-city dwellers, but make no attempt to deal with the naked baby or the bare cabinet?

Why do we feel so guilty after knocking on the doors of inner-city dwellers, but make no attempt to deal with the naked baby or the bare cabinet?

What ties our hands? Why do we feel the tension between social action and evangelism? Who has overcome this tension?

Jesus Healed the Whole Person

Take the example of another man seeking light. He was not in arrears with the local utility company, he was just blind. One man feared a blackened living room, the other came from a dark world. His eyes didn't work, but his ears did. He heard that Jesus was coming. From his spot alongside the Jericho road, he planned his approach. The man in the Coors™ shirt only talked to a preacher. The blind man talked to God. The Memphis man talked about money, utilities, cut offs, and possible darkness. Bartimaeus, the man who approached God, repeated the same words: "Jesus, Son of David, have mercy on me!"

If the man in the Coors™ shirt had cried out for mercy, we would have been confused. If he had come up the church sidewalk crying, "Preacher, have mercy on me!" most of us would not have known what to do. We would have wondered, does he want spiritual counseling and mercy for his sins, or does he have a physical need that maybe we can address? The man at our church door was more specific. "The light bill is not paid. Tomorrow they cut off the power."

When the man with the unpaid electric bill sought out the pastor, the crowd brought him to the preacher. When Bartimaeus sought out Jesus, the crowd tried to hush him up. They rebuked him. Maybe they said something like, "Be quiet. The teacher has better things to do than to listen to your ravings." "Get out of here. You're blind. God must be punishing you for sin. You did this to yourself." "Hush. All you blind people are the same with your constant demands."

Bartimaeus continued his appeal. Perhaps the muffled sounds of a man crying for mercy attracted Jesus' attention. Peering into the crowd for the source of the appeal, Jesus stopped the rebukes with his own: "Call him."

The same people who had pushed Bartimaeus to the back shoved him to the front. The ones who had shouted, "Be quiet!" urged him on with "Take heart." Springing to his feet, throwing his coat into the dust, he groped for the man everybody was watching. As Jesus watched the sightless man approach, he asked, "What do you want me to do for you?"

The blind man gets specific. It's not spiritual mercy he seeks, or safety in paradise, not the promise of a life in the hereafter or membership in the local synagogue. "Master, let me receive my sight."

Then Jesus tells us what he saw when he looked at Bartimaeus. He didn't see a blind man. He didn't see cataracts. He saw faith. "Go your way; your faith has made you well."

Jesus treats the body with the soul.

Jesus treats the body with the soul. He finds a spiritual solution to his physical problem. Rather than sending him away rich in sight but poor in spirit, Jesus uncovers a wealth of faith that results in the gift of sight. Instead of tension between soul and body, Jesus welds the two together. Jesus didn't wonder, "Which is most important? Should I heal or preach?" He didn't treat Bartimaeus as a man divided into body and soul, but as a whole, ministering to all that Bartimaeus requested and needed.

The last line of the story in Mark 10 astounds us: "And immediately he received his sight and followed him on the way." Once he could see, he followed Jesus. Sight back, he focused on the Lord. Physical ailment healed, he sought cure for his soul. Eyes in focus, he looked for God.

What happened to Bartimaeus and the dozens of people that Jesus encountered? Did Bartimaeus stand in the distance as his healer died on the cross? Was he in the crowd on the day of Pentecost? Did he become a disciple? Was there an elder at the Jericho church whose hair was gray, but whose eyes sparkled with youth when he told the children about the day he sat outside of town and Jesus came into his life?

Whatever he became, we know enough about Bartimaeus to conclude that Jesus made a real difference. Whatever happened in the years after their Jericho encounter, we've seen enough to want that same kind of holistic approach in our own ministry. Whatever Bartimaeus saw in the remaining years of his life, we've seen enough in this brief story to realize that we need to be more like Jesus in our approach to people than we've ever been before.

We are seldom as successful as Jesus was with Bartimaeus. We repair someone's house, but while we raise a new wall or fix a bad leak, nobody raises the issue of the soul or fixes a hurting heart. We mass mail spiritual literature into the homes of the poor, but we never see the empty cupboard or notice the barefooted children. In order to be effective, we sometimes refine our ministries into efforts to help people get jobs or a program of aggressive Bible studies for inner-city residents. In the process, we slice up our approach, and the unity Bartimaeus experienced under the expert touch of Jesus disintegrates. They may benefit spiritually or physically, but not both.

We Face the Division of the Physical and Spiritual for Two Reasons

First, we sometimes let the world set our agenda rather than letting Scripture. By this, we mean that, rather than take a holistic approach to ministry as Jesus did, we pattern our ministries after the five divisions of General Motors. Often when we divide our work on the model of the business world, whether for convenience or efficiency, the effect loses touch with the holistic approach of Jesus. We even found that our budget reports betrayed our divided ministries as we listed benevolence under one line item and evangelism under another. Dollars for food and clothes have little to do with funds for spiritual hunger and heavenly raiment.

As we have reflected on our segmented ministries, we often found cloudiness instead of clarity. We've followed marketing directives rather than ministry principles. We have looked to the business world for models rather than to the spiritual world. Books like *The Worldly Church* by Richard Hughes, Michael Weed, and Leonard Allen; and *Resident Aliens* by Stanley Hauerwas and William Willimon revealed more of our secular agenda than we wanted to see.

We learned that our efforts to be efficient and businesslike do not need to divide our faith. Our vision for ministry should run the budget, not vice versa. We must be guided by the biblical vision, not by accounting principles. Instead of being guided by efficiency, we need to be led by faith. While we need to be efficient in the principles that faith dictates, we should not let the principles of faith be dictated by our attempts to be efficient.

Second, we sometimes adopt a worldview that separates the physical from the spiritual. Because of the influence of philosophies like materialism, humanism, and secularism, we separate the physical and spiritual sides of people. Such views are common in our culture:

- ❖ "You don't mix religion (spiritual) and politics (physical)."
- ❖ "The church (spiritual) is not going to tell me what to do with my money (physical)."
- ❖ "Why should I pray (spiritual) before buying a new car (physical)?"
- ❖ "If we just had more money (physical), the problems with the poor (partly spiritual) would be solved."

Although we struggle to maintain a Christian worldview, we often find ourselves thinking like our culture, separating the physical and spiritual aspects of people. Jesus refused to accept this dualism. He argued that the things we have and the spirits we possess are intimately integrated. After warning us not to be materialists, he concludes, "Where your treasure (physical) is, there will be your heart (spiritual) also" (Matt 6:21). Later, after affirming God's concern for their food, clothing, and housing, Jesus states a fundamental principle of Christianity: "Seek first his kingdom and his righteousness (spiritual), and all these things (physical) shall be yours as well" (Matt 6:33).

The danger of dividing the physical and the spiritual is that we end up placing one over the other. Sider is right. Most ministries focus either on the poor *or* on the lost. Jesus focused on both. Our dualism makes us see the priority of either the physical over the spiritual or the soul over the body. Jesus calls us to see the whole man just as he saw the whole Bartimaeus. Only as we overcome our dualistic notions can we hope to treat people holistically.

By making our goals both biblical and holistic, reflecting both the mission and the worldview of Jesus, we hope to imitate his holistic ministry in our own. We offer three biblical ways to maintain unity.

Our Mission Includes Both the Body and the Soul

God's mission included both the spiritual and the physical. God called the prophet Isaiah not only to lead the people to repair the city, but also to restore their souls. Isaiah described his task like this:

> The Spirit of the Lord GOD is upon me,
> Because the LORD has anointed me
> To bring good tidings to the afflicted;
> He has sent me to bind up the brokenhearted,
> To proclaim liberty to the captives,
> And the opening of the prison to those who are bound;
> To proclaim the year of the LORD's favor,
> And the day of vengeance of our God;
> To comfort all who mourn;
> To grant to those who mourn in Zion—
> To give them a garland instead of ashes,

The oil of kindness instead of mourning,
The mantle of praise instead of a faint spirit;
That they may be called oaks of righteousness,
The planting of the LORD, that he may be glorified.
They shall build up the ancient ruins,
They shall raise up the former devastations;
They shall repair the ruined cities,
The devastations of many generations (Isa 61:1-4).

Isaiah's commission mixes the physical and the spiritual. He reports both that the city is rebuilt and that they enter into a covenant with God.

Jesus assumes Isaiah's lofty summons in Luke 4:18 when he quotes the marching orders for his own ministry: "He has anointed me to preach good news to the poor." Jesus had a mission to both. Listen to his vision:

But he said to them, "I must preach the good news of the kingdom of God to the other cities also; for I was sent for this purpose" (Luke 4:43).

Be merciful, even as your Father is merciful (Luke 6:36).

For the Son of man also came not to be served but to serve, and to give his life as a ransom for many (Mark 10:45).

Jesus served people in holistic ways just as he dealt with Bartimaeus as a whole person. He sought to serve people physically and spiritually. Only when we adopt his mission, casting aside our own world-supplied agendas that fracture our ministry, can we hope to find a holistic approach to the lost and the poor. Anyone who claims that the Christian mission includes only the spiritual, needs to read again the simple conclusion of James about spiritual ministry: "Religion that is pure and undefiled before God and the Father is this: to visit orphans and widows in their affliction, and to keep oneself unstained from the world" (Jas 1:27). Any who limit the Christian mission to the physical must note Jesus' own calling: "I must preach the good news of the kingdom of God to the other cities also, for I was sent for this purpose" (Luke 4:43).

Jesus sought to serve people physically and spiritually.

Keeping unity in our mission will help make our ministry like the one Jesus had with Bartimaeus. If our intention is to minister to both, we will more likely achieve a holistic ministry. If we do not have a unity in our purpose, we will not likely find a unity in our effect.

God Loves Both the Body and the Soul

Jesus began the Beatitudes in Luke with God's concern about the poor: "Blessed are the poor, for yours is the kingdom of God. Blessed are you that hunger now, for you shall be satisfied" (Luke 6:20-21). The psalmist expressed God's concern: "The Lord is a refuge for the oppressed, a stronghold in times of trouble" (Psalm 9:9). The three parables in Luke 15 tell of God's love for the lost. The celebrations at the return of the lost sheep, the lost coin, and the lost son tell us how much God cares about lost people.

The celebrations at the return of the lost sheep, the lost coin, and the lost son tell us how much God cares about lost people.

God's love enables him to deal with individuals as a whole. We tend to think in dualistic terms: He is poor, or she is lost. God's love enables him to see the whole picture. Out of that wholeness, he gave Moses a law that dealt with spiritual and physical matters. He sent prophets with the task of instituting justice instead of physical oppression and spreading righteousness in place of spiritual deadness. The twins of righteousness and justice march side by side throughout the Old Testament, reflecting God's total concern for humanity.

Grace Covers Both the Physical and the Spiritual

Ephesians 2 tells us grace covers our spiritual deadness. "But God, who is rich in mercy, out of the great love with which he loved us, even when we were dead through our trespasses, made us alive together with Christ (by grace you have been saved)" (Eph 2:4,5). The salvation of our souls comes through the grace of God. But grace also describes what we do for the poor. The longest section of Scripture about giving describes the special collection for the Jerusalem poor: "We want you to know, brethren, about the grace of God which has been shown to the churches of Macedonia, for in a severe test of affliction, their abundance of joy and their extreme poverty have overflowed in a wealth of liberality on their part" (2 Cor 8:1-2). Later he says that the "generosity of your contribution" was due to the "surpassing grace of God in you" (2 Cor 9:13-14). Their giving was the grace of God.

Grace links both the poor and the lost.

Grace links both the poor and the lost. God ministers to both by his grace. Only when we recognize that the grace of God goes in both directions can we keep our ministries holistic. If we understand that grace saves the lost and grace reaches the poor, then we cannot separate our efforts to the lost and poor.

In the 1930s, a poor family from Texas drove an old car to Tennessee to seek work. They had an accident just outside of Nashville. A child died in the crash. The police called the Central Church of Christ. Christians came to help the injured, to house the survivors, and to bury the child. They conducted a memorial service at their building and then buried the child in a church-owned lot at Spring Hill Cemetery. Such acts of kindness were repeated at the Central Church. Members recall that irate people in the community would call, asking why they spent money on poor people, or why they put tombstones over children who didn't have a penny to their names.

The Central Church secretary knew exactly what to say. She explained, "We believe that even the poor deserve to be buried with dignity." Hear the grace? As the Central Church went about their ministry of helping the poor and preaching the gospel, amazing things happened. In 1929–30, they found jobs for 590 people, provided free housing for 3,222, and served 6,046 free meals at noon. Two church-owned pick-up trucks delivered coal and groceries to the poor in downtown Nashville. A medical and dental clinic in the building served physical needs. Every day at noon, they held a preaching service. From 1925–29, they gave away 275,000 pieces of religious literature. From 1925–45, they baptized over eight thousand people, about one a day.

They weren't perfect people, but their work continues to amaze us. Central Church practiced the fullness of amazing grace, the grace of giving, and the grace of the cross. People responded to their holistic ministry. Stoves were filled with coal, cupboards with bread, and souls with Christ. They never experienced a tension between the lost and the poor because they knew their God aimed to help both, loved both, and offered grace to both.[2]

We continue to experience tension in our own ministries between the lost and the poor. However, we have committed ourselves to striving for a more united focus, to a more holistic approach. In healing the whole person, we hope to be like Jesus.

---

1. Ron Sider, *One-Sided Christianity?* (San Francisco: Harper, 1993), p. 123.

2. Cf. Harold Shank, "Nashville's Central Church of Christ: The First Twenty Years," *Restoration Quarterly* 41.1 (1999): 11-26.

Chapter Six Action Plans

1. Find out what programs there are in your area to help people with financial requests. Call the local Coalition for the Homeless to get you started.

2. Read Mark 10. How do you reconcile Jesus' gift of sight and his emphasis on the spiritual? How would such a combination work in your benevolence outreach?

3. Develop a mission statement that clearly defines your personal belief about giving money and resources to the poor.

4. Investigate what churches in your community have a good reputation for handling benevolence requests. Invite them to speak at a group meeting to discuss their approach and why it works.

Volunteer Ann King stocks the MACS Commodities Closet for Tuesday distribution.

A happy school child leaving the School Store with supplies ready for the first day of school

The homeless often only have one place to turn for help — Jesus.

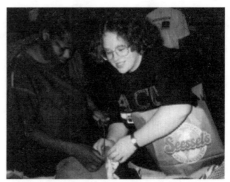

A volunteer helps Rose find clothes at a Clothing Giveaway.

Volunteers (L-R) Pam Byrd, Martha Kee, and Sally Cook share Jesus with inner city children.

CHAPTER 7

Change!

If every single person possessing the capability should assume the care of a single family, there would not be enough poor to go around.

—Nathaniel Rosenau[1]

We were an odd trio. Maybe nobody noticed. Most people in the diner focused on the Southern-style entrees staring up at them from their plates on the Formica-top tables. Feet shuffled across the yellowing tile floor. The motherly waitress seemed impatient with those in the lunch-hour crowd who didn't know the menu by heart like she did.

Trent's enthusiasm for Christ had yet to peak after his conversion to Christ a dozen years ago. His red-hot zeal for God matched the distinctive color of his hair. He had driven his late model car out from his corporate headquarters downtown. From his roomy eleventh-floor corner office, he had a good view both of the river and downtown. From high-rise carpeting to mid-town tile was only part of his journey. He'd left movers and shakers to talk to the moved and shaken. Harold's journey is similar.

My [Harold's] route from a book-lined cubbyhole to the world of Formica, waitresses, and mass-produced home cooking parallels my spiritual journey. A few years before, the trio would have held little interest to me. Spirit-performed heart surgery had given me a new lease on life – and on the particular life we discussed that day.

Mike traveled the farthest and made us the odd trio. A black man breaking cornbread with two whites. A poor man ordering greens with two rich guys. A homeless man squeezing the lemon in his iced tea with two homeowners. A fellow who rode the bus eating with two men who, between them, owned four cars.

Mike's story paralleled his spiritual journey. His parents died, leaving him the family house. As things headed downhill, they picked up speed. He got behind on the utilities, neglected repairs, didn't read the small print on contracts, got in debt, missed payments, and finally lost the house. Jobless, homeless and car-less, Mike ended up bedding down at the Salvation Army. Flipped from one agency to another like the silver ball in a pinball machine, Mike finally heard about "MACS." Mike recalled, "I didn't know what it was."

"MACS" stands for Memphis Area Cooperative Services, the helping arm of area churches of Christ. Together the congregations sponsor a "Life Skills Lab," a commodities closet, furniture distribution, counseling, and referral services. Mike interviewed. MACS accepted him into the next Life Skills Lab, equipping him to reenter productive living. Lab workers put Mike into contact with local Christians like Trent and me.

As we mopped up our greens with buttered cornbread, Mike told us about his two jobs. MACS uncorked his desire to be a social worker. Now he supervises patients on weekends at a local mental health clinic. He transports them and serves in a big brother kind of role. Formerly unemployed and homeless, Mike says, "I get a thrill out of helping the down and out. I tell them God made them all. Nobody is better than anybody else. MACS kept me going. I'm going to help others keep going."

People Can Change

Mike had learned something profoundly biblical. The principle undergirds all that Jesus says: *People can change.* Jesus abruptly told some folks to repent. Others he gently pushed to a better way of life. Jesus' first command? "Repent!" (Mark 1:15). Life doesn't have to be the way it is. Jesus admits nothing about "dogs too old to learn new tricks." When Jesus encountered the "that's-just-the-way-I-am" attitude among religious leaders, he plowed right through. Thick-headed disciples needed two boat miracles and two bread miracles before they saw the point. Mike learned from Jesus at MACS. Now he's out on the streets of the inner city telling others.

When Jesus encountered the "that's-just-the-way-I-am" attitude among religious leaders, he plowed right through.

Trent learned the same lesson on a different level. MACS called one day. "Come down and talk to some of the lab members." Thousands of thoughts raced through his mind. "Will I have time? Will these homeless people have problems I can't handle? Will they resent me? Will they ask me for money? Will they have attitude problems? Can the poor *really* change?"

Lessons Are Taught at MACS

"I walked in and found the lab members at lunch having normal conversations. They weren't calling for revolt. I learned that they wanted to make something of their lives. They were people just like me. I thought I was going to encourage them, but I found I was encouraged.

"Mike and I are just friends. Our culture said we come from different worlds, but God showed us that we have more in common than what separates us."

Mike agreed. Nobody at MACS knew him, yet within days people surrounded him with loving compassion. "It's like a family circle," he said.

93

Trent added, "Knowing Mike has changed me. When I think about new living room furniture, I think, Mike doesn't have any living room furniture. When I wish for a nicer car, I remember that Mike wishes he had a car."

Two men from different worlds finding out how much they need each other. Both benefit from the relationship. Mike is off the street. Trent, now more aware of the influence of his affluence, works extensively among the poor. Together they illustrate how ministries of compassion can change the world.

God Convicts Us of Superiority and Apathy

A twenty-nine-year-old man knocked at the front door of the church building asking for a place to spend the night. Recently fired from his job as backup musician for a traveling entertainment group, smelling of alcohol, stripped of all family and friends, he just needed a place to stay.

I've never been homeless, but I've answered the church door when the homeless called. What do we do when poverty confronts us? I know what I have done, and that is what this book is about. I have sent the homeless on their way with some excuse about not having the proper place or with the encouragement that if he gave up drinking, we could help.

I have sent the homeless on their way with some excuse about not having the proper place or with the encouragement that if he gave up drinking, we could help.

I watched the man in blue-jeans and T-shirt walk down the sidewalk with a naked baby in his arms and my meager ten-dollar bill in his pocket on the way to buy diapers. I've watched ghetto mothers squirm in the receptionist's chair awaiting the arrival of the benevolence deacon to authorize the release of some old clothes from the closet.

I have turned travelers away empty-handed because in my judgment they did not deserve our help. People have walked out of our food closet with less than they needed because we wanted to hoard what was left.

I have preached from Amos but never mentioned the poor. I have asked people to follow Jesus without telling them about his work among the poor, the maimed, the lame, and the blind. I have urged church leaders to put the poor at the bottom of the agenda.

I have asked people to follow Jesus without telling them about his work among the poor, the maimed, the lame, and the blind.

My superiority and apathy troubled me. Superiority because I had work or money which empowered me to withhold from others. Apathy because I didn't try to feel like they felt, but hastily placed blame, rationalized my refusal and rejected their plea.

The twenty-nine-year-old man found a place to stay that night. He knocked on the door of a church that had a heart for the poor. The old Nashville Central Church of Christ gave him a room for the night, asked him to do some housecleaning to pay for his breakfast, and let him stay for six months. He started attending church services, married a young woman in the congregation, became a Christian, and later an outstanding member of the community.

At Central, they believed the demoralized, drunk, desperate man at the door could change. So did Jesus. He did. I've not always felt that way, but God has changed me too.

A few years ago, joining Trent and Mike for lunch would have made no sense to me at all. Filled with misconceptions about the nation's disenfranchised, my understanding of Jesus included nothing about reaching out to the poor. Several events challenged me. We moved. I got a raise. We found ourselves living in one of the poorest cities in America.

Instead of insulating me from the downtrodden, my own economic views began to cut at me. Instead of slicing off the poor like unwanted fat on a piece of meat, my stereotypes about the poor began to expose my own inadequacies. I would later understand that the cutting was the work of God.

Never before had I felt the sharpness of Jesus' words: "I have come to preach good news to the poor" (Luke 4:18). Suddenly his advocacy for the lame, maimed, blind, and poor cut my economic policies into inconsistent bits of American capitalism and myopic Bible study. From prison, I sent word to Jesus like John did. "Are you he who is to come, or shall we look for another?" (Luke 7:19). John's reaction is not recorded, but mine is vividly remembered. Each word pinned me to the back of my self-made cell as I listened to Jesus' response:

> The blind receive their sight, the lame walk, lepers are cleansed and the deaf hear, the dead are raised up and the poor have good news preached to them (Luke 7:22).

Each text I encountered sliced away at my previous views. Each Scripture became a battleground where God brought about change in me. Each lesson I studied revealed that I had been imprisoned by unchristian attitudes and unbiblical perspectives.

Suddenly jail cells started slamming shut everywhere. One day after morning services a tearful young mother from a nearby church told me how she and several other mothers taught the Bible to some children on the "bad" side of town. After several weeks, the church elders there told her, "Quit doing that. It's not the job of the church." Clang, a prison door slammed shut.

I met a couple from a large Midwestern church at the hospital room of their ill child. They told how they had started an outreach to a small group of Asian refugees. Classes filled up. People got involved. But others in the church complained, "We don't want them in our church." Clang, another cell door slammed shut.

A good friend returned from her home congregation. Several of her friends had started a class for handicapped children on Sunday morning. The children responded well. People eagerly volunteered to help. Then some complained that the handicapped children distracted their worship to God. Church leaders stopped the program. Clang.

One bright Sunday morning, a Hispanic man in blue jeans and flannel shirt stood in an area of a large urban church called the patio as five hundred people filed by on their way from Bible classes to the assembly. The patio should have been called the Jericho road. Nobody stopped to help. Clang, the key turned coldly on another cell door.

A man spoke about the biblical mandate to help the poor. Back in the crowd an anonymous voice whispered, "Well, that ought to satisfy the bleeding hearts." Clang.

Behind each bar, I saw my face staring back at me. The bars of misconception and the security of stereotypes had kept me from seeing the message of Jesus, from responding to his call to "preach the good news to the poor."

Jesus Leads Our Journey

You see the road Harold traveled to reach that lunch-time conversation. Now we travel together. You may be slightly ahead, perhaps we're ahead of you. It's not a race. It's a journey. Jesus leads our expedition. The desperate calls of the downtrodden pose difficulties for many travelers. Some would rather not make the journey. Fortunately our guide is a good one.

He took me to meet Jacqueline Smith, who sleeps on the street by choice. Sleeping bag by night, lawn chair by day, she keeps watch over the Memphis Lorraine Motel, now the National Civil Rights Museum, where a bullet killed Martin Luther King, Jr., in 1968. Her sidewalk protest demonstrates the need for housing for the poor. She feels that the museum only made more people homeless.

One humid Memphis day, we asked her about her church background. Although she grew up in our Christian tradition, she maintains only a distant connection with two of our congregations. When asked what we could do for her and the homeless families and children in Memphis, she said, "Maybe your churches could let our poor children feel the cool air inside your air-conditioned buildings. It might encourage them to do better."

All people can change through the power of God.

Jacqueline understands Jesus. He calls us "to do better." Demands to improve can be bad news, but with Jesus the call is good news. Good news because all people can change through the power of God. No prison can withstand his explosive, freeing power. No lock can restrain his vision of human liberty. Changes are wrought through the work of a dreamer.

- ❖ The twenty-nine-year-old Nashville man changed.
- ❖ Homeless and unemployed Mike now works two jobs and supports his own apartment.
- ❖ Formerly wrapped up in the sophisticated agendas of the corporate world, Trent now spends time each week working with the Life Skills Lab.
- ❖ Trapped in a prison of self-importance, cinder block walls of bad thinking keeping us from showing compassion, we, too, are evidence of Jesus' power to change people.

We have done wrong. Each biblical text raised in this book has been a personal battleground where God has slain those wrong attitudes and altered our priorities. He put the guards to sleep and led us out the front gates of our prison. Repentance is never easy, but it is possible.

Poverty surrounds all of us. Beggars confront downtown workers. Rough hands clutch the cardboard sign reading "Will Work for Food" outside shopping malls. A ragged family in a rusted-out station wagon parks down the block in order to go door to door seeking work.

If the poor do not contact us face to face, awareness of poverty comes through the newspaper or television. Pictures of lower-class families driven out of their homes by a flooded river or images of nearly naked people in African deserts with distended stomachs mar the television screen. Statistics about people who can't pay their rent or the increasing numbers on welfare stare at us from the pages of the morning paper. Poverty confronts us all.

If the poor do not contact us face to face, awareness of poverty comes through the newspaper or television.

It Gets Us Down Unless We Remember Two Things

First, the poor can change. Pessimistic thinking about personal prognosis doesn't come from the Bible. Jesus based his whole ministry on the assumption that change can occur in human character. Transformations unfold in the Gospels as Jesus ministered to the poor and the rich.

Jesus sings the harmony of hope as he marches to the chant of change. He dreams about how things might be because he knows how they can be. Where we see prison walls, he sees open fields. Our eyes sense the darkness, his eyes penetrate to the light. Repent! Change! Alter! Correct! Convert! His marching song drowns out those who sing the dirge of rigidity and the lament of limitation.

Second, we can change. Trent did. Harold did. We all have. People respond differently to society's outcasts. Some get angry with the poor. Others avoid thinking about the downtrodden. Poverty depresses some people. Some blame the poor for their own problems. A few redefine the disenfranchised to suit their own liking. Each response creates its own prison cell.

Jesus models life for the Christian. Read the Gospels. He lived among outsiders. He cared for the poor. He served the down and out. He adopted the disenfranchised.

Many imagine that Jesus is just like us. He must be a white-collar professional, well educated, suitably dressed, and socially aware. We impose our suburban values on him. We force him into our stereo-types. We made him in our image.

Milton Jones, who preaches in Seattle, tells of passing out peanut butter sandwiches to the homeless people on Skid Row. Lumbermen used to skid logs from the mountains down to the ocean in the area where the city's poor now live.

A homeless man with peanut butter sandwich in hand poked Milton in the ribs. "I know you. You're Milton Jones. Why, you're the last person I'd expect to see on Skid Row." Milton had no idea how the man knew his name.

A week later, Milton listened to a Christian call-in talk show on the car radio. The moderator posed this question, "If Jesus came to Seattle today, where would he go first?" Callers agreed that Jesus would go directly to Skid Row.

Milton was stunned. Why was it that the first place everybody expected Jesus to go was the last place anybody expected Milton to go?

Perhaps it's appropriate to begin this chapter in an urban diner and end up handing out sandwiches on Skid Row. The journey began and ended with a change of venue. Harold made the journey, just as Trent and Mike did. We've all followed the same path. It's an expedition we invite you to join.

If being like Jesus means anything to you, let him pry open the bars of your heart to the poor.

If being like Jesus means anything to you, let him pry open the bars of your heart to the poor. Evaluate your prison cell. Examine your perspectives. Surely we can eat and travel together.

---

1. Nathaniel Rosenau, *23rd Annual Report, United Hebrew Charities* (New York: Seixasm, 1898), p. 20. Cited in Marvin Olasky, *The Tragedy of American Compassion* (Wheaton: Crossway, 1992), p. 225.

Chapter Seven Action Plans

1. Find out what job training programs are available in your community for the poor.

2. Read the book of Amos through in one sitting. Write down your insights into what Amos says about compassion.

3. Volunteer with a local agency that teaches reading skills to the illiterate.

Students gather for group at Memphis Area Cooperative Services Spirituality Class.

Life Skills Lab instructor Katherine Moore leads a "life map" discussion at MACS.

Veronica Matthews congratulates Deborah on completing her GED at The Downtown Church.

A happy moment at a MACS graduation with Verlon Harp, Dir., and Katherine Moore, Life Skills Lab instructor

---

Nothing Succeeds Like Success

> The question is not, 'How do we help the poor?' but 'How do the poor themselves escape poverty?'
>
> —Viv Grigg[1]

Neighborhood mothers handed their children over to the day care worker named Kathy. Do-it-yourselfers rented their equipment from the counterman named Larry. Struggling alcoholics shared their problems with Bill, a certified counselor. The college professor called on a promising student named Donna.

What do Kathy, Larry, Bill, and Donna have in common? They were all once chronically unemployed. One was homeless. Another was in prison. All in a mess. Each one headed for disaster. Then they went through our "Life Skills Lab," which we will describe below. Now they fully support themselves, and their future is rolling down the track. That's not always been the case in our work. Let Ron tell you about the experience he and a church benevolence committee had with Angelina.

Angelina Revealed the Need for a Better Way

We were tired. Tired of poor people making requests we couldn't handle. Tired of doling out the meager resources given to the benevolence committee. Tired of trying to verify the stories.

We were worn out. Worn out being the benevolence police. Worn out passing judgment on people we hardly knew. Worn out waiting for people to come to us. Worn out reacting rather than acting.

Angelina gave us new life. She came asking for a job. We were elated! Tired of determining who was worthy of help and who wasn't, Angelina excited us because she wanted work rather than welfare. We agreed to help. Two scanned the newspaper's "help wanted" section, another called church members who owned businesses, and a couple checked with the employment services. In less than a week, we found three solid leads. We took turns driving Angelina to interviews.

Then a dry-cleaning chain called. A job! She started Monday! We were more excited than Angelina. It seemed so easy. Give the unemployed a few good leads and ZAP! Instant success! Bolstered by that success, we made the initial step toward starting a job pool from the church membership. It went so well for the next few days.

Then the other shoe fell.

Angelina lost her job. She explained that the baby got sick. She stayed home from work two days, but didn't call in on the second day. When she returned on Thursday, the manager had given her slot to someone else.

She didn't know she needed to call in *every day* when the baby was sick. After all, she called once. Besides, she didn't like the atmosphere. The boss demeaned her. Coworkers made rude remarks. One man even made a pass at her.

We were more upset than Angelina. She wanted us to crank up our job-finding machine again. We agreed. Perhaps the dry cleaning position wasn't her kind of job. Within the week, Angelina was back at work. By the next weekend, she quit. We found a third job. She lost it in less than a month.

We were tired again. We questioned our approach to finding jobs. Maybe Angelina wasn't ready to work. Should we refuse to help her until she's "serious about working"? How do we decide when *that* will be?

Our failure with the whole benevolence program and our frustration at our triple failure with Angelina divided us into two camps. Half of the committee members struggled with guilt. The others boiled with anger. Ron felt both.

My [Ron's] internal guilt wondered what we did wrong. Every sentence began with "if only." "If only we had prepared her better." "If only we had found the right job." "If only we could make the system work for Angelina." Deserting Angelina, leaving her two children with an unemployed mother, burdened us with more guilt.

I also felt anger. Angelina betrayed us. We played the role of the miffed mother, angry when our "child" failed us. Angelina's failure reflected on our character, our values, and our record. The bad report card embarrassed the whole family. We did our "Christian duty," helping a poor woman find work. We concluded, "Poor people are poor because they just don't want to work." We determined to screen prospective families to avoid this failure. Pick the right people. Be more successful.

While we tired, the benevolence committee at another church struggled with a similar difficulty. They operated a small shelter for women. It solved temporary problems, but offered nothing permanent. Few moved from dependence to self-sufficiency. Most ended back where they started. Abused women returned to their husbands. The unemployed remained jobless. The addicts stayed addicted.

Both ministries sensed something was missing. Our experiences linked poverty and the inability to find and keep jobs. We wondered what stood behind their difficulties in holding a job, so we dug deeper. Should we take a more holistic approach? What about God? How could a poor person draw up a realistic plan for career development? Where could we find a relevant model?

One Program Answers the Job Dilemma

One night, the shelter's director saw a news clip about a program in New York City that taught homeless people how to choose, find, get, and keep good jobs. Called "HOPE," it boasted a seventy percent success rate. Any program that put seventy percent of its graduates in the job market looked like a solution to our weariness. The director was ecstatic. His enthusiasm provided a surprising direction for the churches of our own city.

The idea behind the program was simple. Start small, fourteen-week classes to teach people basic life skills. Let them learn about themselves first. Let them answer the question, "Who am I, and where do I want to go?" Many urban Americans never ask those questions. It just doesn't seem relevant to their world. Philosophical pondering over existential questions doesn't rank high on the daily "To Do" list.

Second, teach them to match their personal interests and abilities with their work. After students examine hundreds of different jobs and careers, they learn how to locate information about the career field that *they have chosen.* Investigation follows, with a strong emphasis on planning for a lifetime career, not just a job.

After six weeks of full-time study, the class breaks into two parts. Each morning for eight weeks, students volunteer at a job internship in their chosen field. Here they learn what the job of their dreams is like. Fantasy meets reality. The work so appealing in the TV ad may be less glamorous in real life. After working for three hours in the morning, they return for an afternoon of classroom instruction, honing their job-keeping skills, writing resumes and letters of introduction, learning to get along with difficult coworkers, handling problems in the workplace, and addressing personal issues through counseling. Finally, a graduation party honors the students as they receive their diplomas. For many, it's the first time they have ever completed anything significant in their lives.

With some alteration, New York City's "HOPE" program provided a framework for our own ministry through Memphis Area Cooperative Services (MACS). The New York City program focused on job security, not spiritual security. With impressive results in the employment field, this secular approach did nothing to direct the homeless toward Christ. In the end, the graduates thanked the program, not the Lord. We added a spiritual emphasis to the classes, with weekly spiritual discussions, daily devotionals, and a volunteer Christian staff, and called the program the "Life Skills Lab" (LSL). Local churches sponsored the work, with the first class graduating in the summer of 1990. By the end of 1994, nearly one hundred homeless and chronically unemployed people received their diplomas. More than seventy percent continued to work a year after graduation! Though LSL was not overtly evangelistic, more than ten percent of the students became Christians, or rededicated their lives to God!

Over ten years of work with the Life Skills Lab doesn't make us experts in helping people construct careers, but we've learned how to lay the right foundation so that the structure remains secure. Our building thrives in part because it benefits both the LSL students and those in the churches who sponsor and volunteer. Both groups together build a structure neither group could build individually. That structure is built around four basic cornerstones.

Cornerstones for a Firm Foundation

One cornerstone is dignity. During those roller coaster weeks in 1990, Angelina failed at three jobs in six weeks. We failed in our three attempts to aid Angelina. One problem in our relationship with her was the lack of dignity. We tried to fix Angelina's problem. We assumed the solution was within the group, not Angelina. We asked, "What can we do to help her?" Equating *compassion* with *handouts,* we solved her problem but lost the opportunity to give her the dignity of finding her own solution. Helping people with money or a quick job search, or a place to stay for the night, or a bag of groceries almost always ends in failure. Treat the poor as if they are helpless, and they will usually be helpless. Condescension and pity cripple the poor.

Helping people with money or a quick job search, or a place to stay for the night, or a bag of groceries almost always ends in failure.

The Life Skills Lab is based on dignity. From the beginning of the interview process, we treat students with care. The staff members are called coordinators, not teachers, to encourage equality. We walk beside them as they find the path best for them — not in front of them or behind them. The role model for the Life Skills Lab staff comes from Jesus, the servant, who washed his disciples' feet. While maintaining his place as their teacher, he encouraged them to "become like their teacher." Dignity means accepting our students as adults capable of making their own decisions about their lives, job choice, and family.

A second cornerstone is loyalty. When Angelina failed the third time, we started looking for someone with more potential. Guilt and anger had blinded us to Angelina's problem. It was not that Angelina couldn't *find* work, but that Angelina didn't know *how* to work. Urban children grow up with few role models for job identity. Inner-city role models include pimps and crack dealers, not teachers and businesspeople. Inner-city children see a single parent living on a monthly welfare check, not a working parent. No one prepared Angelina to earn a living. Unaware, we dropped Angelina. That's exactly what she didn't need.

The inner-city people may lack job keeping skills, but not loyalty. Poor people seldom are able to translate the strong sense of loyalty into a job-keeping tool. The Life Skills Lab focuses on that sense of community as fundamental in helping people reconstruct their lives. The Lab is a minicommunity. As the lab members develop a sense of unity, students intuitively realize their interdependence.

Working with a group of ten or twelve adults for eight hours a day, five days a week teaches all of the students to get along with one another. Tensions arise between group members and the staff, or between cliques within the group. By helping students work through their interpersonal problems in a group dynamic structure like the Life Skills Lab, we teach the value of teamwork in the workplace.

In the first week of class, the group draws up an agreement. When they sign the agreement, they commit themselves to the group.

When one member drops the class, the group feels sadness and anger. The dropout hurts the group, not just the staff. Lab members say the group becomes "like a family." They share struggles and conflicts with the group they've never shared before. By using the natural sense of community in the inner city, the Lab member learns about loyalty — both being faithful to another and having people committed to them. Loyalty makes a big difference in keeping a job.

A third cornerstone is forgiveness. Helping students apologize when they are wrong teaches a humility that preserves dignity. When they apologize, they apologize for what they did wrong, not for their existence. Modeling this kind of behavior has been one of our most instructive tools. Yet Ron knows it hasn't been easy.

One Lab member named Burt and I [Ron] were at odds with one another on a minor issue. During the argument, Burt stormed out of the classroom. I followed him down the hallway, challenging him to stand up to me and tell me what was making him so mad. I pushed every button to provoke a response. Refusing to talk, he left the building.

I returned to the group frustrated and angry. I remembered our philosophy of treating everyone equally. When two Lab members tangled like Burt and I did, I would ask the group to comment on what they saw. Swallowing my pride, I invited the group to comment on my argument with Burt. Their responses surprised me. They said I was harsh and combative. I didn't allow Burt to speak. I didn't treat him like a man. I acted like a bully.

I was shattered, but glad the group had focused on the problem. Later I apologized for my outburst. The next day, after we had resolved our differences, we told the group. They were impressed. It was a new experience for them. Two grown men from two different cultures. One white and one black. Reconciled and standing arm in arm. Both smiling!

Burt and I still didn't agree on the issue, but we discussed it as two mature adults and resolved the conflict and our relationship. Forgiveness requested, offered, and received.

The first casualty of poverty is hope.

A fourth cornerstone is hope. The first casualty of poverty is hope. For the poor, hope does not spring eternal, so hope is the first thing to restore as they begin to manage their own lives. Hope creates the possibility of change.

Before lunch one day, the staff praised one Lab member for her work on a job search report. As the group members joined in by pointing to the positive aspects of her report, she began to sob softly to herself. She said, "That's the first time in my life that anyone has ever told me I did *anything* good." Forty-five years old, but never received praise for her work. Imagine! Nearly half a century without positive affirmation.

There are no grades in the Life Skills Lab, no comparisons between class members that promote self-deprecating analysis. Instead, each student is evaluated on their progress, not their potential. This is not a technique of "dumbing down," but one of "smartening up." An atmosphere of nonjudgmental learning, encouraged by a cohesive group of supportive class members, promotes accelerated learning. Many poor people know only a revolving door of failure: at school, at home, in their personal lives, at the workplace. The last thing they need in an introductory course to life skills is a curriculum that marks their progress with a potential for C's, D's, and F's.

When Angelina came to our church for a job, our reaction was typical. We immediately accepted Angelina's assessment of her need — to find work — and set about the task of finding her what she wanted. We failed to understand Angelina before we started up the job-finding machine. If we had asked, we would have learned that Angelina had never held a job for more than six months in her whole life. We would have discovered that she came from a family that did not work. She had no role models on which to base her hopes for success. The classic mistake of benevolence ministries is trying to fix things for other people before they really know what's broken.

The Life Skills Lab concept stands on a foundation that leads us into partnership with the poor. Partnerships work for people like Angelina, who need not just a job but a whole new view of life. And such partnerships are good for those who help because we're no longer benevolence police tired of repeated failure. We are now delighted friends watching our new acquaintances enjoy their new lease on life.

Ironic, isn't it? The things that stand between people and a good job are simple things like dignity, loyalty, forgiveness, and hope. Angelina needed all four. We supplied job leads, but no dignity. We offered rides to various interviews, but no loyalty. We provided a list of phone numbers, but no spirit of forgiveness. We helped for a month, but gave her no hope.

Angelina is still out there, probably living on welfare, struggling to survive. Through the Life Skills Lab, people like Angelina can find what they really need and what God's people can really offer.

---

1. Viv Grigg, "Church of the Poor," in *Discipling the City*, Roger S. Greenway, ed. (Grand Rapids: Baker, 1992), p. 167.

Chapter Eight Action Plans

1. Encourage your benevolence minister, deacon, or ministry leader of your church. Take him out to lunch, and ask him to tell you about the people he deals with. Ask how you can help.

2. Read Richard Batey's *Jesus and the Poor* (New York: Harper and Row, 1972). Write an action plan based on its contents.

3. Confront your own prejudices about the unemployed poor. What assumptions do you make about them? List ways that this chapter helps you to challenge those assumptions.

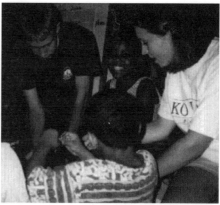

KidsCamp volunteers teaching camper Lakeisha a craft as she learns about God

One child prayed, "Lord, please keep me alive tonight, 'cause there's so much shootin' in my neighborhood." Children often die young in the city.

Ayana loved swimming with KidsCamp. Families and children are at the heart of our work in the city.

Inner city children gather every Sunday morning for Bible class at The Downtown Church.

Teacher Veronica Matthews hosts Parents Day for her Sunday School students.

CHAPTER 9

Making a Difference Makes a Difference

If we wipe out poverty but neglect to tell the poor the Good News about Jesus Christ, we will have failed in our mission. And if we preach the gospel but ignore the plight of the poor, we are false prophets.

—Roger S. Greenway[1]

It was a marvelous day in the inner city. Johnnie Mae looked stunning as she came down the church aisle in the midst of the inner city. George's smile radiated over the entire audience as he waited to welcome his bride. As they met in front of the preacher, they looked lovingly into each other's eyes. They promised to love forever. They promised nothing would interfere. They promised it would never end.

Something interfered. It ended. "Forever" lasted three months.

The spring night air invigorated all of us, but not as much as Tracy and Yatisha. The two girls, who for three years walked the streets of "Prostitute Row," now promised to walk with the Lord. Instead of loving whoever had money to pay, they committed to love the man who paid it all. The church family beamed over how the power of God had broken the power of Satan. Their nighttime baptism not only confirmed their faith, it reinforced the faith of the whole church. Christ removed their impurity. Christ offered them the way. Christ gave them a new life.

Three weeks later they returned to the night life. They went the wrong way. After all, impurity paid the bills.

Larry amazed all of us. The fourteen-year-old learned his lessons well. The Sunday school teachers at the inner-city church said he was the star of their show. His shining face reflected the purity of his life. In an atmosphere of juvenile rebellion, he gave his life to the church. In a society that prized the immediate, he looked to the future. We began to pray he would be our first "home-raised" inner-city evangelist. The handwriting on the wall was all positive.

The headline announced his arrest. "Home raised" inner-city dope dealer. The future dimmed. End of story?

No. George and Johnnie Mae got back together and back with church. For four wonderful months, George led singing, even presented his first sermon. Johnnie worked at her first job and loved it. We trusted them with a key to the church building. Things started missing. A coffee-maker. Two folding chairs. A stapler.

Then George and Johnnie Mae started missing. Like the office items, they were gone. Five months later, she called from the emergency room with her head split open to the bone and her marriage split to the core. Fearful of George's anger, she pleaded with us to help her find a safe place on the outside. Over the next few weeks, George entered an anger management program, Johnnie Mae got the house in order, and they celebrated their first anniversary with their third reconciliation.

Tracy, Yatisha, and Larry have the same bouncing story. Between stints of selling their bodies, the girls return crushed and penitent to their church family. Larry tearfully tells the terrible story of his hated drug dealing two or three times each year. He changes with the weather.

As we said in the first chapter, life in an inner-city church is like a roller coaster. There are those moments of pure joy when the car plunges to the bottom. A few seconds later, we wonder if we'll ever get back up to the top of the hill.

Why are the victories of the inner city so short-lived?

We expect the ups and downs in life. We expect the stock market to soar and plunge. We expect the weather to change. We expect the river to be up in the spring and down in the fall. But why are the victories of the inner city so short-lived?

Little Is Permanent on the Mean Streets

The cycles we've experienced with George, Johnnie Mae, Tracy, Yatisha, Larry, and others like them reflect the roller coaster culture of the inner city. While people in the suburbs say the only certainties of life are death and taxes, people in the ghetto say the only changeless part of life is food stamps and the first day of school. Everything else is like the fog that burns off by mid-morning. Anthony's visit with Stella and her brother Miko is proof.

Stella lives in a shotgun house with a rotten floor. Miko put planks over a couple of the holes. There's no money for repairs. There's little hope for anything better. Both wait for the monthly letter containing food stamps and AFDC. Stella has three children, Miko knows of two who are his own. We met them through a clothing giveaway at the Downtown Church. Although they attend infrequently, they still consider the congregation their spiritual home, and Anthony the best of their new friends.

After Stella served warm juice, I (Anthony) told them about my dream to plant several churches through Memphis Urban Ministry around our city like the Downtown Church. I talked in lofty terms about God calling me to this task. Before I could paint in the details, Stella, with a refreshing boldness, interrupted me.

"Would you shut up talkin' 'bout leavin'?"

115

Telling the preacher to shut up is rude, even in the inner city. "Do what?"

"Anthony, stop talkin' that way. Our daddies leave us, our preachers fail us, and we can't even count on our mommas half the time. We ain't got nuthin' permanent in our lives. Anthony, you've got to stay."

Telling the preacher to shut up is rude, even in the inner city.

Miko's words burned themselves into my memory. He said, "The only reason people keep comin' to the Downtown Church is because you've stayed. So don't be talkin' about leavin', talk about stayin'."

When Anthony told us that story, it reminded us of all the permanent parts of our lives. Our fathers have lifelong commitments to our mothers. We've been surrounded by reliable family, faithful friends, consistent schools, reliable ministers. Part of the routine of our lives is that little changes. If it does, it's because we've chosen it.

For Stella and Miko, everything changes. Their father left when they were babies. They lived three years with one aunt and two more with a cousin. In the past six years, they have lived in nine different houses. Stella has been with four different men. Miko has had three women. Stella never graduated from high school. From seventh grade to the time she dropped out in tenth grade, she walked the halls of six different schools. Miko worked one job for four months. In the past six months, he's collected paychecks at three different places. Once, he lived under a bridge for six months eating pigeons and whatever else he could find.

In one year, Stella went to government offices five different times because they kept changing her status. She's had so many social workers that they all start looking the same. In the last three years, five churches met in one storefront near their home.

The whirlpool of change sucks Stella and Miko into its neverending sinkhole. Powerless to overcome it, they often find themselves precipitating even more change. So late one night, they plead with an inner-city minister not to leave. His four-year presence in their neighborhood has been one of the most permanent aspects of their lives.

Most Inner-city People Live Only for the Present

Johnnie Mae and George never plan a day ahead. The money in their pocket should be spent today. Tomorrow isn't real. The weekend is a lifetime away. Why think about supper when there's not much for breakfast. Why plan for tonight when there's nothing to do right now? George and Johnnie Mae allow events to drive their lives. They don't plan the day, they react to what happens. They don't set the agenda, they try to survive the agenda that unfolds.

As inner-city workers, we teach the Bible to bring light into dark lives. Trying to set an appointment for a Bible study can be frustrating. We'll agree on a time with Johnnie Mae and George only to arrive at an empty apartment. If we have appointments set up with four people for a Thursday afternoon, only two of them show up.

The other side of this roller coaster is that we can teach without appointments. Simply traveling through the neighborhood, we find several "spur of the moment" Bible studies, visits, and prayer times.

Living in an environment that responds to the moment leaves many urban dwellers unprepared for the future. Johnnie Mae and George roll with the waves. Their on/off relationship with God reflects their own response to each day's events. George and Johnnie Mae have much more to contend with in getting to church on Sunday morning than we do. The fact that they continually return to church reflects an attempt to escape that cultural prison. Along with impermanence and living for the moment, another part of urban life is more threatening.

Not long ago, we noticed how thin Johnnie Mae had become. Weight loss is a sign of crack use. Drugs are like dominoes for Johnnie. She uses because she's depressed. She's depressed because she is lonely. She's lonely because she's forced George out. She

117

forced George out because of his anger. This cycle characterizes many of the inner-city people we know.

Violence dominates the inner city. Children hear pistol shots through their bedroom walls. Every day, some man beats on a woman whose screams are unheeded. Teenage boys seek manhood through anger and vengeance. Unnoticed women dress to get noticed only to get raped and robbed in a dark alley on the way home from the store. Desperate mothers scream at even more desperate children. An elementary school child in one Memphis public school was asked, "What is the greatest problem facing children in your city?" The youngster didn't hesitate.

"Death."

It's hard to stay upbeat in a violent world. Depression can drive a person to many things in the inner city. George beats Johnnie Mae. She crawls to our door, begging us to help her and the kids into an abuse shelter. He tearfully begs one of our ministers to help him get his family back, promising to do something about his anger. She comes home on a promise with the seventeen stitches on her forehead yet to be removed. The cycle starts again. We don't see them for awhile. Then they come, needing a light bill paid. Inside we throw up our hands realizing that conflict and confrontation is part of their daily routine.

In our inner-city church, we teach that, if a person won't stay and work out a problem between brothers or sisters, then the Spirit of Christ is not in him. Though painful to us, our ministry grows through the struggle. *Staying* is what God has done with us. *Staying* means, "I will never leave you. I'm willing to do whatever it takes to keep this relationship."

Confrontation has its sweet moments. Two sisters argue over how to run the clothing giveaway. Others rallied around the two upset women. The two mended the breach one Sunday morning during "Testimony Time" as they walked from opposite ends of the room to hug and apologize. The church that witnessed their conflict joined in their celebration.

Another negative factor powering the inner-city roller coaster is the long history of broken family relationships. Our first impression of the inner city included the complicated household relationships. In her lifetime one woman may live with several men along with children from several families. Eleven- and twelve-year-old girls have babies. Babies raising babies. Daughters are expected to raise their siblings, and sons are taught that they only need to make babies. Dysfunctional relationships abound. Children growing up in such confusion repeat the cycle in their adult lives.

Annie lives with Marvin. Neither is married, to each other or anybody else. Three children are theirs. Another two are hers and one is his. Three other children belong to her younger sister who lives down the street with a man who is not the father of any of the three. His kids live in North Memphis.

Most of the people we've mentioned either come from similar homes or know such environments intimately. Chaotic families produce chaotic people. Breaking the cycle is never easy.

Chaotic families produce chaotic people. Breaking the cycle is never easy.

Wanda lives with Terrell, who beats her and cheats on her. Terrell steals from her to support his habit and sleeps with her when he wants. Wanda stays with Terrell because Terrell is all she has. Her father deserted her, her mother is dead, her two sons are in gangs, and she has no friend she can trust. As undesirable as he is, Terrell is her friend.

Like all of us, Wanda wants to be loved, accepted, and appreciated. She gets those things occasionally from Terrell, but nobody else. Until she came to know Christ. For six months, Wanda said little about Terrell, but then in a tender moment she pleaded for help to escape her awful life. Sinful? Yes. Unproductive? Yes. Easy to escape? Not for most inner-city dwellers who seek love and affection like all humans.

The roller coaster life of inner-city people perplexes most new-comers. Even when we understand the impermanence of their lives, why they live for the moment, confront the violence of their culture, and recognize the fragile nature of inner-city family life, we often despair at how to help them survive, spiritually and physically, in this kind of world.

God shows people life at its best through the church. In the church, God's community seeks a higher standard, speaks of hope in the midst of despair, cries with those in pain, and points to a clear authority. In some ways, it's easier to be a church in the inner city, because godly living stands in such contrast to much of the culture. It's easier because people of the inner city more readily confess their faults. It's easier because the need is so apparent.

The inner-city church is Robert's island of sanity. He lives in a boarding house filled with mentally ill men who refuse to take their medicine but replace their pain with a rock of crack. He sees the worst of life before his morning coffee. But Sunday morning opens another world. The ears that hear cursing on Saturday hear praising on Sunday. The eyes that see debauchery on the downstairs couch see holy people in folding chairs. Walls covered with cutouts from porno-graphic magazines are replaced with walls covered with murals of Jesus rising from the dead.

He sees the worst of life before his morning coffee.

Robert's church experience gives him stability in a changing world. For three hours he looks to eternity in a world that seldom sees beyond lunch. He experiences peace before returning to the violent streets. He hangs onto his adopted family before reentering the chaotic family of his youth. The church is the brakeman that slows his roller coaster ride. It helps him through the valleys by pointing out the difference between good and bad. Without the church, his life is out of control. With the church, he experiences the most consistent part of his week.

At church, he accepts all people, a drastic contrast to the racist environment he calls home. At church, he learns that God loves the poor, contrasting with the greed of his larger world. At church, he understands that even the weak can help the strong, differing from the dog-eat-dog world. At church, he senses community, not the world's "every man for himself." At church, he gives sacrificially, but returns to a boarding house full of hoarders. At church, he confesses his weakness, while nobody shows weakness on the streets. For Robert, church allows him to enter, for a moment, a different world, and that makes a difference in the world of the streets.

In his book *Race,* Studs Terkel quotes black historian Lerone Bennett, Jr.:

> Given the way we were forced to live in this society, the miracle is not that so many families are broken, but that so many are still together. That so many black fathers are still at home. That so many black women are still raising good children. It is the incredible toughness and resilience in people that gives me hope.[2]

That's not a message we hear on the ten o'clock news during their series on inner-city crime. In the roller coaster ride of the inner city, it's remarkable that many families stay together at all.

Mrs. Bea was baptized in the Tallahassee River over thirty years ago. Her life has been one of ups and downs. She lived through the racial riots, marched with civil rights protesters, and lived just around the corner the night Martin Luther King was shot. She's had a companion who constantly berates and threatens her, telling her that she's no good. The only permanent thing in her life was her mother. She could always count on momma, until momma died. When it happened, a big part of Bea died also. She contemplated suicide. She got a gun to do the job, but couldn't go through with it because it belonged to her son. She didn't want him to feel responsible for any part of what she wanted to do. She got another gun, but that's when her friend Bobbie invited her to the Downtown Church. Mrs. Bea found warmth, love, and new family members. She attends church faithfully, serves at the Clothing Giveaways, helps make decisions in the church meetings, and travels with the church on "road trips." Mrs. Bea is living again because the void has been filled. She has something permanent in her life again. The emptiness that she felt when her mother left has been replaced by an overflowing sense of daily presence by brothers and sisters in a loving church. Church family gives her strength to stand up to her abusive companion. Being with God's family helps reorient her own family relationships. Knowing God is always there helps her to have the courage to *stay*, when it would have been easier to leave. Mrs. Bea says, "If it wasn't for the Downtown Church, I'd be dead right now."

"If it wasn't for the Downtown Church, I'd be dead right now."

Donald Thomas lived on the street for several years, staying in the shelters when it was cold. We became acquainted with Donald and helped him through our Life Skills Lab. At graduation, he took the podium to talk about one person or one group that he appreciated more than any other. He called the name of our church and gave us a plaque that hangs in one of our offices. He wrote this poem:

> We stand here, with no place to go.
> > They try to assume our status quo.
> The strangers walk by and give us a stare;
> > very few of these people even seem to care.
> As I start walking, the snow begins falling.
> > The blessed passersby continue their malling.
> I feel the slush through shoes that have holes.
> > The crowd stampedes by with an upturned nose.
> To say the least, my stomach cramps from hunger,
> > and as a result my mind starts to wander.
> Just for a place to rest my head,
> > some place warm with a nice cozy bed.
> As my feet start aching from standing all day,
> > again my mind starts to drift away

As I consider the skills that I know,
> the fact remains: I have no place to go.
I ponder the fortunate that have a home;
> I often wonder if they ever feel alone.
But on a night such as this you soon realize
> that the Almighty's watching with very concerned eyes.
For I soon discover a vacant abode.
> It isn't luxurious, but it eases my load.
I give thanks to the Father and ponder the morn
> and soon fall asleep, for I'm comfortable and warm.
Before I know it, it's soon breaking day,
> but my strength is renewed, for the Lord made a way.

Donald has hit higher highs and lower lows than most people we know. Yet deep inside, this man knows a better way, a more stable life. Knowing Donald's difficult life and sensing his incredible faith touches all of us. Making a difference makes a difference. Knowing that teaching people about God makes a difference builds us up.

---

1. Roger S. Greenway, *Cities: Mission's New Frontier* (Grand Rapids: Baker, 1989), p. 50.

2. Studs Terkel, *Race: How Blacks and Whites Think and Feel about the American Obsession* (New York: The New Press, 1992), p. 10.

Chapter Nine Action Plans

1. Go back through this chapter and write down the main points. Then write down your first reaction to them.

2. Cut out articles from your local newspaper for one week that deal with violence in your community.

3. Pray against violence in your city daily.

4. Visit an inner-city church one Sunday morning. Get there early to meet the people that come in. Ask them what their community needs.

Life Skills Lab graduate Brenda now works for Rural/Metro Ambulance
Service while training to become an Emergency Medical Technician.

Life Skills Lab Instructor Katherine Moore
congratulates a new graduate.

MACS graduate Latausha, who is
congratulated by sponsor Elise Parham,
learned of the Lab at the School Store.

Verlon Harp (left) and Ron Bergeron (right) congratulate a Life Skills Lab graduate.

CHAPTER 10

There's Profit in Partnership

One of the most valuable gifts you can offer your street
friends is to assist them in decision making.
—Gray Temple, Jr.[1]

Barbourinski's Institute for Racial Harmony
Advises Memphis

The tiny nation of Barbourinski in Eastern Europe seldom makes
the news. The name was unknown to most Memphians until three
citizens arrived in West Tennessee. Barbourinski's Institute for Racial
Harmony sent them to Memphis because of our long history of racial
tension. The echoes of the sniper's gunshot that killed Martin Luther
King, Jr., reverberated even through the Iron Curtain.

The Institute for Racial Harmony (IRH) represented two cen-
turies of resolving racial conflicts. After bloody wars between the
Eastern Solecks and the Barbours in the eighteenth century, they put
racism behind and lived in perfect harmony. Now they wanted to
share with us.

We'll never forget those initial meetings. The representatives of
IRH told a large congress of influential Memphians we were doing it

all wrong. Barbourinskian Sergey Hellinxyc offered an angry critique of our religious, social, economic, and political structures. Another unveiled a series of overheads outlining the new way the races would relate in Memphis. Certain populations would move. Churches needed reorganization. The proposed political apparatus reflected an Eastern European structure. They presented a new economic initiative. No one seemed untouched by their radical proposals.

As they presented their agenda for the religious community, we felt a growing outrage. They ignored long-established religious differences. Some of their plans offended our most prized spiritual sensitivities. We shook our heads, thinking this will never work here. These people from IRH don't know our city, we thought. How can they impose order on our society without asking for our input? Decades of history enter into the equation. How do they know their plans will work for us?

As they plowed over our principles, feelings, history, and sensitivities, we noticed other Memphians responding in the same way. Instead of harmony, they created hostility. Instead of wanting to work with them, we wanted them to go home. How could people achieve unanimity in their home nation but create such animosity in ours?

Nothing they suggested worked. No plan was approved. Nobody rose to their support. Aside from our momentary unity in opposing them, they left our community worse than they found it. When the three boarded the Air Barbour flight to Sendicow, our whole community sighed in relief.

Never heard of Barbourinski? Unaware of the Institute for Racial Harmony? Sleep through the fiasco in Memphis?

No, you didn't miss anything. We made it up. The fictitious tale of the Barbourinski reverses the roles. Normally, Americans travel to needy lands. We send missionaries to the Third World. Peace Corps volunteers jet to remote corners of the globe. Our military invades to support democracy. Our music plays on radios in Brazil and Belize. American books sell in stalls from Cairo to Copenhagen.

Americans are used to sharing our ideas with others. We've done it for years.

We've seldom received a delegation from Barbourinski. We don't understand the reluctance of others to accept our ideas because we have seldom been in a situation to be reluctant to accept the ideas of others. Used to giving, we're unfamiliar with receiving.

Get the point?

Invade the inner city like the military landed in Haiti, and expect problems. Act like the Barbourinski delegation, expect a Memphis-type rejection. Only when we put ourselves on the receiving end can we understand how inner-city people see the delegation from the suburbs.

We might welcome the delegation from Barbourinski as *partners,* but not as dictators. We willingly hear their story, but also want them to hear ours. We might care more about them if they seemed to care more about us.

The Inner City Recognizes True Caring

Now listen to a true story. When we saw the headline, our hearts sank. As a church, we struggled for years to launch partnerships with inner-city people. After months of building relationships, after earning the right to be heard, and maintaining a presence in Foote Homes for weeks, we, the outsiders, felt some camaraderie with the insiders to poverty.

The headline declared: "Churches Take Message to Projects." A four-column picture showed the minister of a large suburban congregation in the city talking to a woman from the projects. Before outlining the favorable response from the inner-city neighborhood, the reporter quoted that minister: "We want these people to know that just because they live here, that doesn't mean nobody cares about them."

How could this other church be so successful after one day of door knocking in the same community where we had pounded the pavement for eighteen months? Glad that another group soared while we crept, we wondered if we needed a new direction.

At a meeting the next day, Anthony surprised us with his upbeat mood. Confused because they were not down in the dumps with us, we pulled out the newspaper story to pop their balloon.

"I've seen that."

"You have?"

"Those people come to the projects once a year. They knock on every door and go home. The residents say nice things to the reporters on the streets, but inside their apartments, everybody laughs at them. People in the projects know the difference between people out for publicity or a warm fuzzy feeling and those people who really care." Anthony had learned about partnership.

We understood. Our slow burn approach didn't make the headlines, but it did make dinner table conversation in Foote Homes. Attempts to heal the brokenness with a door-knocking blitz made great reports at some suburban Sunday night service, but left gaping holes in inner-city hearts.

Attempts to heal the brokenness with a door-knocking blitz made great reports at some suburban Sunday night service, but left gaping holes in inner-city hearts.

The one-day blitz of this suburban church changed perspective as we looked through the eyes, not of a newspaper reporter, but of our inner-city ministers. It showed us the shortcomings of our own one-day efforts. A single day's invasion doesn't win much of a war. Rather than a triumphant invading army freeing the oppressed, the door knockers seemed to resemble the royalty on a fox hunt. Pose for the pictures so we can get home in time for supper.

Ways That Make a Difference among the Poor

Both stories raise questions. Can we make a difference among the poor? How can we make that difference? After putting in hours of planning, after recruiting all the volunteers, after months of traveling to the inner city, can we expect to see any real changes in the people and the way they live their lives? Do we do any good at all? The answer depends on two things: how we define the "we," and what we mean by "make a difference."

Who Are the "We"?

Can people from the suburbs solve inner-city problems? No. Can outsiders provide what poor people need? No. Left up to the Barbourinskians among us, we'll not make much progress. The trail between the suburbs and the inner cities is littered with broken dreams and failed social programs. Poverty has expanded, not decreased in the urban centers of America despite huge financial investments. Invading Barbourinskians seldom succeed. Door-knocking blitzes provide only Band-Aids™ for inner-city malignancies.

Door-knocking blitzes provide only Band-Aids™ for inner-city malignancies.

Imposed solutions seldom work. A fix to the problem outlined at a Washington conference table or a suburban church meeting will not transform the inner city. A partnership forged between the haves and have nots in Chicago will probably not have the same results if imposed on the poor of Miami.

Partnerships will make progress. When we work as partners, both the outsider and insider can benefit. If we knock on doors one Sunday afternoon, it may make us think we've done our duty, but it provides little service to the other's need to be helped. A Christmas blanket may warm our hearts, and it might insulate an inner-city body, but it will do little for an inner-city soul. Ministry is never an advertising blitz. It's not a photo op. Affecting lives means a slow, steady, constant presence in the arena of their struggles.

If the "we" includes "us" and "them," then "we" can make a difference. Togetherness in planning, praying, and programming will lead to greater progress in accomplishments, achievements, and acceptance. Partnership with inner-city people means making the effort to understand the obstacles they face in life. How we approach those obstacles determines whether we make any "difference."

What Makes the "Difference"?

Tom approached an inner-city church mission as a preteen. Too poor to afford shoes during the steamy Memphis summer, he arrived barefoot. A hastily formed church committee huddled briefly. They decided "no shoes, no service." Tom left and didn't return to any church for the next twenty years. Rejected. Scarred. The suburbanite decision-makers thought they were raising standards in the inner city. In reality, they imposed their standards on our young friend, like the Barbourinskians did on Memphis. Tom's case is repeated constantly. *Visitors* to the inner city make a difference. A negative one.

A political science professor told us the unwritten goal of most social programs is to keep the poor from rioting and burning. If that is the only difference we want to make, then most any aid to the city will keep the mobs at home and fires at bay. Those programs make a negative difference.

If, however, we mean a positive difference in the lives of disenfranchised people, then the answer depends on the attitude of the people involved.

If, however, we mean a positive difference in the lives of disenfranchised people, then the answer depends on the attitude of the people involved. Suburbanites lose enthusiasm quickly. Change in the inner city comes slowly. The "warm fuzzy" feeling of a Saturday doorknocking blitz disappears when the long process of transforming lives begins. Inner-city people live discouraged lives because poverty puts up more barriers than they can overcome. Failed quick-fix programs force them deeper into dependency and frustration.

It takes both sides to win the fight over discouragement. Most outsiders will give up unless they recognize some of the frustrating aspects of inner-city life. A few of the chief frustrations illustrate the issue.

Simple tasks aren't so simple. Alex Kotlowitz, in *There Are No Children Here,* tells a typical project mother's story. Although she tried to be a good mother, her poverty created too many barriers to overcome. The nearest grocery store was two miles away. She had no car. She could make multiple trips on the bus and hand carry her purchases, or she could take a taxi home with the groceries for a $6.25 per mile cab fare. Lack of transportation complicated the simple task of putting food on the table.

We can pick up a gallon of milk and a head of lettuce and still be home in time to catch Dan Rather. Simple tasks like shopping can paralyze an inner-city resident.

Washing and drying clothes is a snap in the suburbs. We cannot remember the last time we were forced to use a laundromat. Most women in the projects wash their clothes in the bathtub. Others frequent clothing give-aways to get free clothing. The family will wear these clothes until they are too dirty and simply discard them. There is little or no money for the washeteria, even if there was one nearby. To make a difference means understanding the daily struggles of inner-city people.

Obstacles wear away perseverance. It takes the three of us an average of five minutes to get to our offices. Between our three families, we have seven cars. We can be anywhere in the metropolitan area in twenty minutes.

Adrienne Walker, a single mother living in the Cleveland inner city, finally got a job at a Stop-N-Shop™ in the suburbs. Her friend's promise to provide transportation faded after a few days. Three hours one way on the bus seemed overwhelming, especially with the complaints from her ailing grandmother who kept Adrienne's year-old son. Adrienne quit. She encountered substantially greater obstacles in getting to work than the three of us combined.

The continual barricades faced by inner-city residents wear out their "want to." Getting to work becomes harder than the work. Signing up for school is a greater test than the classwork itself. The multiple roadblocks reduce inner-city perseverance.

Few poor people feel loved or secure. People need love, affection, meaningful work, and security. We usually get our needs met. Many poor people go *years* without having these needs met. As a result, their lives are chaotic.

One news report told of a California man who remembered the Depression poverty of his youth. Many poor people during the Depression were highly motivated people who had no opportunity. The man could not understand why today's inner-city people don't care. He calls them "the 4-D people," folks who are dope pushers, dope addicts, drunkards, and dropouts. According to a news report, he was one of 1,500 demonstrators in Santa Cruz in 1990 who protested against the homeless in their community. Panhandling, sleeping in parks, and petty theft caused many communities to pass laws regulating and restricting homeless and poor people. Newspapers called it "compassion fatigue."

Not much love or security is there? The poor get blamed for many ills in society. Violent crime in the inner city suggests that those in poverty often lash out at others in the same situation. Loveless lives, hate rather than affection, meaningless work, and constant exposure to violence characterize the daily routine of our poor friends.

We've felt just like the California man. We've been frustrated with our inner-city comrades. But as we've become their friends and now understand the daily dilemmas they face, our frustration has faded, and our fatigue has transformed into energy.

Frustration ranks high on both sides. Suburbanites don't accomplish much because they don't understand the barriers posed by inner-city life. They often see only tax dollars wasted, laziness, and poor motivation. The disenfranchised see only the big houses and expensive cars in the suburbs. Partnership bridges the gap, opens hearts, and reforms minds.

A life of poverty is filled with endless bureaucracy. Lilly wanted to complete her GED. She filled out four forms in order to take a leave from her job and three forms to gain entrance to a GED class at a local high school. She was assigned to a school fifteen miles from her home. She applied for a transfer by filling out two more forms and, after waiting in line for three hours, was given a place in a classroom four miles away. She walked two miles to stand in line one hour to get bus tokens for the first two classes. She'll have to repeat the process for the remaining classes. On her first day of GED class, the teacher said they were out of books, but that an agency in south Memphis (four miles away) would lend one to anybody with a valid driver's license. Lilly's driver's license had expired because she didn't have the cash to renew it. The motor vehicle registration office was only open during the hours she worked. She missed a day's pay to stand in line to get her license renewed, only to find out that she'd have to come back because she had the wrong papers.

Inner-city people face such barriers every week, complicating their lives, removing their dignity, and stifling their spirit.

Inner-city people face such barriers every week, complicating their lives, removing their dignity, and stifling their spirit. Discoveries like these have made us more sympathetic to the plight of the poor. Our increased sympathy has created in us a spirit of partnership. We work arm in arm with our inner-city friends, and together we whittle away at the endless poverty and injustice of the American inner city. Can we really make a difference? Yes, we can.

---

1. Gray Temple, Jr., *52 Ways to Help Homeless People* (Nashville: Nelson, 1991), p. 50.

Chapter Ten Action Plans

1. Consider a long-term plan to reach an inner-city neighborhood. Reconsider any quick "clean-up day" projects your church has scheduled. Focus on the long-term.

2. Visit outreach centers in the inner city with a small group of interested friends. Talk afterwards about what you see.

3. Take a bus or train ride through your city. How would it feel to be without a dependable car to get around in?

4. Go through a food stamp line with a poor person or visit the local food stamp office and observe the people there. What insights do you gain into their lives?

CHAPTER 11

A Tour of the Future

> If at this moment in history a few million Christians in afflu-
> ent nations dare to join hands with the poor around world, we
> will decisively influence the course of world history.
>
> —Ron Sider[1]

Where does all this effort among the poor end? Let's go on a trip.
Turn the tour bus toward the city for a sightseeing tour of the future.
Not the tomorrow we'll never see, nor the future of a distant century,
but the future of the next decade. Not a future we can barely imagine
and never influence, rather one we can picture and possibly create.
Let us tell you what we see and what we think the future could be.

We Are Disturbed by the Present Reality

Take the tour bus past the nation's subdivisions hidden behind
the cedar fences, beyond the beehive-like shopping centers with cars
buzzing around the honeycomb of shops, past the straight streets of
pristine neighborhoods filled with towering oaks, beyond the out-
skirts of the city toward the urban center. Don't go to the glass-walled
canyons of downtown. Stop short of the sports stadium. Slow down
before you reach the Crowne Plaza. Stop somewhere between where

the corporate leaders work and where they live. Pull over in a spot sandwiched between the special occasion restaurants lining the city's downtown streets and the suburban kitchens where families enjoy their evening delights. Stop at the real city.

We know its name: The Ghetto, The Slum, Skid Row, The 'Hood. We know what it looks like. Old houses with sagging roofs and broken sidewalks line up the streets like wounded soldiers answering roll call. Beer bottles in the gutters and stinking trash barrels litter the urban war zone. Broken windows, abandoned cars, a soiled love seat with its cushions exposed rank among the casualties of battle. It's the home of the poor and the land of the despised.

We See the Future Possibility

But as we pull the tour bus off the freeway, our imagined future explodes before us. We see not the present reality, but the future possibility. We're shocked! It's not what we expected. The future "ghetto" is not like the present reality. Newly shingled dwellings look down on sidewalks like perfect white ribbons along the street. Neatly clothed neighborhood children zip back and forth like toy cars with new batteries. Reflections from the living room windows catch the contours of the freshly painted front porch furniture.

As our dream-powered tour bus moves down the street, our apprehension changes to astonishment, our dread to delight, and our doubts to dreams. The Ghetto has changed. The inner city has not become suburbia, but the Ghetto is gone. From the front seat of the tour bus, the cycle of American poverty looks broken. Thinking we have stumbled into an isolated model community, we search other notorious streets only to see a smile on the new face of the American city.

The Ghetto gone? The inner city changed? How? When?

The transition of ghetto to gold, of Skid Row to Park Place took years. Victories occurred with people more than with places. The transformation of hearts preceded the metamorphosis of the neighborhood.

One day the mayor announced a cutback in police protection, not because of a budget shortfall, but because of a drop in crime. Drugs disappeared from the streets. Dealers found the territory increasingly "dangerous" to market. Nocturnal businesses selling instant satisfaction of sensual desires saw potential business dry up. "Action News" chronicled the clean-up of the American city. The local paper lauded the transformation of the Ghetto from a jungle to a neighborhood. All fingers pointed to one cause. Which one do you think rewrote the Ghetto's future?

- ❖ Huge government programs financed out of Washington.
- ❖ Massive input of funds from the corporate world.
- ❖ Revolutionary new curricula in the public schools.
- ❖ Benevolent efforts by an organization of professional sports figures.
- ❖ New laws that curbed crime.
- ❖ Refurbished court systems and prisons.

Each played a role, but in our dream the media, government officials, corporate leaders, education experts, and other public figures credit one influence: *spiritual renewal.*

The media, government officials, corporate leaders, education experts, and other public figures credit one influence: *spiritual renewal.*

Our tour bus jolts to a stop. Spiritual renewal as in "church"? Spiritual renewal as in Christianity? Before you write us off as daydreamers rather than visionaries, before you slam down this book wondering if you can get your money back, listen to our case.

Jesus Dared to Dream

We dream this dream because Jesus dreamed it. Maybe our drive to the inner city has its unreasonable aspects. Maybe we've seen the future too much through our own eyes. Maybe we've made the inner city look too much like suburbia. But we dream because he dreamed.

Nobody dreamed like Jesus. He glanced at Simon and saw Peter. Looking at Levi, he imagined Matthew. As he walked by the lanky Galileans with fish guts clinging to their clothes, he saw the leaders of a worldwide spiritual revival. From hick towns in Palestine, he dreamed of a kingdom that would conquer Rome.

Jesus had to be a visionary.

He had to be a visionary. How else can we account for the Christian movement? What explains how Christianity became the largest peacetime revolution in human history? What powered millions of people against all odds to carry his word to every continent? Jesus set the vision. He dreamed the dream.

He had to be a dreamer. Anybody who could take us where we were and make us into what he says we are has to have vision. How could anybody look at sinners like us, racked with wickedness and filled with failure, and think, "With these, I can change the world"?

He saw things we can't see until we begin to look as he looked. See what he saw. When he saw people darting aimlessly around life's hillsides like frightened sheep, he dreamed of a shepherd calling them to order and taking them home. He asked simple, Palestinian peasants to live the highest moral system ever established. He called twelve men to stretch higher than they ever thought they could reach.

He was a dreamer. Look at his vision when it comes to Skid Row and Ghetto City:

> Blessed are you poor, for yours is the kingdom of God.
> Blessed are you that hunger now, for you shall be satisfied.
> Blessed are you that weep now, for you shall laugh (Luke 6:20-21).

Did Jesus give the kingdom of God to the poor? Don't Christians own the kingdom? How could Jesus envision a time when the hungry would be fed? Most think the hungry will never be fed. Why did Jesus dream about the bereaved laughing? Only people watching comedians laugh.

Not according to the dreamer. He took the dream tour of Skid Row long before we ever heard of a tour bus. He saw beyond the shantytowns of Latin America and food lines of Africa and slums of America to a different kind of world.

Jesus' Disciples Carried Out the Dream

Was it just a dream? Look at the book of Acts. Look at the dreamed-of kingdom in action. Hungry people whisked off the street. Look at the sign on the corner:

Lot for Sale
Contact Barnabas
Must Sell
Need Money for Worthy Cause

Lines of people donating money. The rich sharing with the poor. The spirits of giver and receiver transformed. A whole new world order of poor folks leading the kingdom of God, of satisfied hungry people, of laughing weepers.

He dreamed about a change in the way the world viewed the poor. He dreamed of people having a change of heart toward business as usual. He dreamed of bag ladies sitting at the kingdom's main banquet table. He dreamed of homeless people sleeping in the master bedroom. He dreamed of a spiritual upheaval in society that would shake down the rich and elevate the poor.

Even his mother dreamed his dreams. Before he was born, Mary sang this song:

> He has put down the mighty from their thrones,
> and exalted those of low degree,
> he has filled the hungry with good things,
> and the rich he has sent empty away (Luke 1:52-53).

What a child! What a dreamer! From cradle to cross, Jesus upset the status quo with visions of a new tomorrow. Not only did he dream, but he brought his dream to reality in his own ministry, in the dynamic outreach of the Jerusalem church, and even in our own day.

Can we dream his dream today? Will it work? Can the bus tour of America's inner city come true?

Remember the story in chapter 6? In the Depression days, a small group of Nashville Christians caught a sense of Jesus' dream. They loaded their Bibles and families into their Fords for the drive to downtown Nashville with a vision of making a difference among the poor in their city. Working as the Central Church of Christ, they set up a medical clinic, a dental clinic, a free noon meal, and a day care program for working mothers. They served over 45,000 hot meals from 1925 to 1928. Add on another 6,000 for lunch in 1930. They refurbished a five-story hotel for women without homes and added three floors on their church building to house men. Christians delivered groceries, clothes, and coal in the church pickup trucks.

Tucked between a dance hall and a prize fight arena, surrounded by all the shady sensual dealings of street life was the tiny Central Church. Soon prostitutes fed on God instead of prowling males. Poor people found food for stomach and soul. The dance hall closed. Couldn't stand the competition. The prize fight arena moved. Had to find a different clientele. Peek at an old newspaper clipping quoting the Nashville Chamber of Commerce:

> There is nothing pretentious and grand about this wonderful church. It is simple and appealing, just the kind of place that both the fortunate and the unfortunate like to go for spiritual comfort, and within is found those with their hearts in the work, and who grasp the hand of him in rags and tatters and make him feel as much at home as the man in finer dress; where the woman of the underworld and the primrose path is as welcome as the woman in finery and splendor. The new institution has become a wonderful power in the civic life of the city of Nashville through its simplicity and whole-heartedness. . . . In reality, the church is a civic center, and any and all are welcome.[2]

Sounds like somebody listened to a dreamer. Sounds like somebody took a drive in their Model T and saw a new kind of city. Urban renewal not by the government, not through education, not by corporate donations, but through spiritual renewal.

Today Christians from Los Angeles to Houston, from New York to Memphis find the dream still alive. New inner-city churches, Life Skills Labs, after-school programs, classes with teenage girls, and distribution programs for the homeless feed on the dreamer.

Can the inner city of our bus tour become a reality? Can we break the serious cycles of crime, hunger, substandard housing, broken families, substance abuse, cracked infrastructures, high infant mortality rates, disregard for education, racism, homelessness, unemployment, and the like? Can the ghetto of tomorrow become a place where God's kingdom reigns among satisfied, happy people? Will Jesus' dream work? Yes!

Three Reasons That Jesus' Dream Can Work

First, Jesus identified the central problem. A wealthy, first-century Baby Boomer asked Jesus about living forever. In his response Jesus put his finger on the human problem: "No one is good but God alone" (Luke 18:19).

None of us measures up on the "good" scale. Nobody in government or education is good, not a corporate manager nor a university professor. All of us come up short. From suburbs to Skid Row, from the Galleria to the Ghetto, nobody hits a hundred on the good scale. The central problem of America's inner city is sin.

Despite our bad track record, Jesus dreamed of a different world. He envisioned whole communities of people who were good as a result of God's work, not by their own efforts. He looked at lost people and saw saved people. He looked at bad people and dreamed about good people. He saw people who hit bottom on the good scale and longed for them to score a hundred.

Spiritual renewal sets the foundation for all other renewal. Without addressing the central human issue, all other attempts repeatedly hit the wall without making much of a dent.

Think about the American slum: crime, drugs, broken families, depressed mothers, demoralized fathers, discouraged children, empty lives, blank futures. Like the rest of town, America's inner city ranks low on the good scale. Sin touches nearly every inner-city issue.

Sin touches nearly every inner-city issue.

Jesus addressed sin. Listen to the precision of his mission statement: "For the Son of Man came to seek and save the lost" (Luke 19:10). Jesus knew how to fix the sin problem. He fixed it then. He can fix it now.

Memphis has a program called Responsible Adolescent Parenthood (RAP). Designed for young girls, it aims to keep unwed teenage mothers from having a second child. After sitting in on the sessions, over ninety percent of the girls never have a second child outside marriage. How do they do it? Counselors tell the girls not to get pregnant. Most of them have never heard that message! What spiritual group sponsors this program? The U.S. Government.

If government can bring about that kind of change through socially-oriented counseling, imagine what Jesus could do if his people worked with the same kids. Unwed, teenage mothers need spiritual advice. Unemployed fathers need spiritual help. Homeless people need Jesus. Poor people need to know that the dreamer said that they own the kingdom! Jesus' dream will work because he identified the central problem.

Second, Jesus' dream provides unlimited resources. That jolts us. Where's the bank account? Show me the warehouse. What kind of unlimited resources? Helping the poor takes money. Lots of it. How will this dream be funded?

George Bush's inaugural address discussed the social issues in America. At one point he said we had the *will* but not the *resources* to solve the problems. One of the news commentators after the speech disagreed. He reversed what the President said. He argued we have the *resources,* but not the *will.*

The commentator hit a profoundly spiritual note. Jesus provides the most crucial element in changing people: the *will*. Altering the inner-city calls for resources. Money, food, building supplies, education, training, the list goes on. But the Dreamer didn't leave us a Swiss bank account or a warehouse on the south side. He didn't because we need the *will* more than the *resources*.

Jesus insisted, "Be merciful, even as your Father is merciful" (Luke 6:36). Not coins and materials, but compassion and mercy. People with money don't always help. People with mercy are driven to serve. The missing ingredient is the *will*. America's inner city can change when the people have the will to change it.

America's inner city can change when the people have the will to change it.

Jesus provides that *will*. He supplies all of his dreamers with unlimited sources of compassion, mercy, and love. His spring of kindness never runs dry. The cross of Christ towers above the glass giants of downtown, showering unlimited supplies of love on all who will receive. The cross of Christ spreads beyond the sprawling subdivisions of suburbia, offering carloads of compassion from people who dream with the dreamer.

Imagine a spiritual army with an unlimited supply line of love marching into the war-torn inner cities of America, launching missiles of mercy, and firing salvos of compassion. Think of the damage that explosions of mercy could do to inner-city crime. Spiritual shrapnel pierce each home. War horses of wickedness retreat in surprise. The evil ranks flee in confusion. In the aftermath of the battle, the forces of good help create a new world order, a new inner city, a fulfillment of an age-old dream. Jesus provides the ammunition.

Third, Jesus provided the dreamers. Did Peter and John still smell like fish when they presided over the massive distribution program of the Jerusalem church? The Galileans had gone from frequent

143

fishing to daily distribution. Matthew reversed directions, from taking money in to giving it out.

One verse of the Jerusalem church story is absolutely amazing:

> There was not a needy person among them, for as many as were possessors of lands or houses sold them, and brought the proceeds of what was sold and laid it at the apostle's feet; and distribution was made to each as they had need (Acts 4:34-35).

Did you hear it? "Not a needy person among them." Poverty solved! Ghetto closed!

Jerusalem attracted poor people like garage sales lure bargain hunters. Religious folks on the way to the temple wanted to keep all the Old Testament laws about giving to the poor. The needy of Palestine stationed themselves at the temple gates to receive their last minute donations.

Yet within the same city another worldview attracted huge crowds. Rich and poor fell at the feet of Jesus. Inspired by his dream, they erased the inequities. They found ways to plug all the holes. They fed every mouth. They fixed every problem. They resolved every shortcoming.

What happened in Jerusalem was planned in heaven. Jesus laid out the boundaries in his own ministry: "For the Son of man also came not to be served but to serve, and to give his life as a ransom for many" (Mark 10:45).

The Lord served. God became a slave. The ruler washed feet. The top man did the dirty work. Kingdom language and kingdom principles created kingdom people. Kingdom people turned the status quo inside out and upside down. They did it by serving.

Servants fill the ranks in the kingdom's army. Victories are won by the foot-washing crowd. Just as Jesus came to live among us to serve us, we live among those who need to be served. Staying in the suburbs won't cut it in this kingdom. The Dreamer wants the tour bus *moving* on the road.

Spiritual renewal and spiritual revival can break out in America's ghetto. A host of urban problems stem from untreated sin.

People with unlimited sources of compassion can realign the forces of the Ghetto. Servants can bring about change.

Servants can bring about change.

It's happened before. Just ask people in Nashville in 1930. Some of them are still around. It *can* happen again.

---

1. Ron Sider, *Rich Christians in an Age of Hunger*, 3rd ed. (Dallas: Word, 1990), p. 215.
2. Cited in A.M. Burton, *Gleanings* (Nashville: Life and Casualty Insurance Co., 1932).

Chapter Eleven Action Plans

1. Ride with a police officer one afternoon on his regular beat.
2. Pray for inner-city leaders from among their own people. Encourage a local inner-city preacher in his efforts by sending him a note telling him you are praying for him.
3. Form a group to investigate your church's history in dealing with benevolence requests. Ask the leaders how you can get involved.
4. Volunteer at an alcohol and drug treatment program for the indigent.

Volunteer Sally Shank asks Linda
at a Clothing Giveaway
if she would like a Bible study.

Life Skills Lab Counselor Ron Bergeron
takes a lunch break with a student.

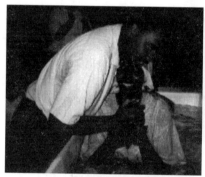

Apprentice Pat Pugh raises Mary up
out of the waters of baptism.

Anthony Wood passes the leadership of
The Downtown Church to Jeffrey Matthews.

Downtown Church members prepare supplies for the annual School
Store. Highland St. has served over 50,000 children with supplies.

CHAPTER 12

Parting Advice

*But this essay is not about pessimism. Quite the contrary, it is
about the remarkable hope being rekindled in communities across
America. Faith communities are at the center of this good work.*
—Henry G. Cisneros[1]

We remember watching the evening news. As the camera panned the crime scene, the anchorman said, "Another shooting at a north side housing project raises the city's crime rate to the highest level in five years. The mayor responds. Those stories and more coming up on Action News 5."

We remember driving by the "Will Work for Food" signs at the local mall, wondering, "Will they really work?" "Was it a con?" "Could we get hurt?"

We remember seeing the homeless woman outside the downtown theater. We shuddered as she pawed through the overflowing dumpsters next to the Crowne Plaza Hotel.

We remember feeling ripped off by the welfare programs, reading the repeated reports about the increasing number of people on public assistance, and doubting that we could do any better than the bureaucrats.

We remember.

We remember being like other churches doing little about the poor, even disclaiming any church responsibility for helping, wondering what the 350,000 local churches in America could do to end poverty. We wondered how to change the hearts of indifferent church leaders, then realized sometimes we *were* those reluctant church leaders.

We wondered how to change the hearts of indifferent church leaders, then realized sometimes we *were* those reluctant church leaders.

We remember committing ourselves to the poor, while realizing we didn't have a clue about how to solve poverty, how to fix the awful way that people had to live, or how to help without being ripped off.

We remember.

We remember failing. Starting over. Failing. Starting over. We remember being rejected, conned, used, and cheated by the people we tried to help. We recall the fear at hearing gunshots and the repulsion at seeing the wounds. We remember the despair when nothing seemed to work, nobody seemed to care, and no hope was in sight.

We remember the joyful faces of poverty-stricken, inner-city kids, the tears of the welfare mothers, the good confession of the dope addict. We remember the bar that closed, the miser who gave, and the inmate who said, "This is the first thing I've ever finished in my life." We remember the bonding between the rich woman and the poor mother. We remember.

That's why we write.

We have no degrees in mercy, no diplomas in wisdom, no long years of experience. We have one qualification for writing: We remember what it was like to start. We recall being first graders in the school of serving the poor. We remember the questions, the uncertainties, the fears, the premonitions of failure. We passed first grade and now sit across the hall in second, but we've not forgotten those issues that initially plagued us.

We Started with Shaky First Steps

Starting out is hard. The first step in helping the poor often brings confusion and frustration. We remember crawling when the world of the poor and unfortunate seemed alien and dangerous. We remember our first faltering steps.

We walked into a room full of confusing options. The literature about social justice and social action is vast and confusing. Theological thickets abound. Sociological treatises about helping the poor often omit the concerns of God himself. The needs of the poor quickly overwhelm sensitive hearts.

We walked into the world of the urban underclass. Poverty in the American city differs from rural problems or third-world issues or middle-class difficulties. Violence escalates. Families disintegrate. Racism flares. Moral values plummet. Corruption reigns. The novice enters a new world.

Despite the problems and the ever-present obstacles, what we remember most of all is hope.

We walked into a world of hope. Despite the problems and the ever-present obstacles, what we remember most of all is hope. As we walked among the poor, our hope of making a difference grew. We found promise on a bleak landscape because we learned that we were not alone, that others had preceded us, that the poor were a helpful source of direction, that the more we knew about our city the better we served, and that God opened doors as we prayed.

We Took a Peek Backstage

A few years back, we opened the morning paper to the headline: "Local Church Announces Move to the Suburbs." The story followed the set pattern: "We can't find anybody to minister to in the city." Then the evening news announced more cuts in medical services to the poor. That discouraged us. Like Elijah, we felt pretty much alone. We thought nobody cared about the poor. We felt helpless.

Then we discovered, despite the bad press, that many people want to help, they're just waiting for someone to ask them to help. We asked. They helped. Soon we had 10,000 volunteer hours in just one of our ministries. Another ministry had too many volunteers. When specific needs arose, Christians offered transportation, dental services, medical care, catered lunches, extra clothing, Christmas presents. The list seemed endless.

One Sunday night, we asked our congregation to write out prayers for the poor. We braced ourselves for a measured response, hoping that maybe twenty-five of six hundred people would participate. On Monday morning, we counted over three hundred thoughtful prayers about the oppressed. Many Christians repented of their insensitivity. Others sought forgiveness for greed and covetousness. Many pled for guidance about serving those less fortunate than themselves. Reading through the prayers of our brothers and sisters moved us to repent of our bitter sense that nobody was interested in the poor.

Prayers are not the only way to monitor interest in the lowly. We've coined the phrase "Hallway Money," referring to funds given in the hallways of the church building. As needs among the poor became known, the "hallway money" flowed. One ministry collected over $20,000 of hallway money in just eight weeks. Hallway money and "special contributions," one-Sunday contributions, have funded our ministries over the past ten years.

We thought we were alone. Nobody cared. But just as in the days of Elisha, God pulled back the curtain to reveal backstage support (2 Kings 6).

We Discovered a Long Line

We thought we were the first ones to face such confusion. Then we realized we stood in a long line. That isolationist view seems silly now, but it was real then. We weren't the first first graders. We walked well-worn paths.

Before starting a ministry among the poor, we joined in other efforts. We helped with the local Meals-on-Wheels, worked in the Big Brother program, and served in soup kitchens. As we networked with the pros, we met people from our own church who worked professionally with needy people: social workers, abuse counselors, service providers to the elderly, day care supervisors, nurses, doctors, and others. We became partners in serving the poor.

The most encouraging experiences came from visiting other ministries.

The most encouraging experiences came from visiting other ministries. An eleven-year-old, inner-city ministry in Nashville filled us with dreams of a better Memphis. A six-year-old effort among the homeless in Houston stretched our minds about what might be done. A simple one-day idea we read about in a newspaper became a wonderfully successful means of showing compassion.

Working with others lowered our confusion index. As we networked across the nation and throughout our city, our hopes grew and our knowledge multiplied as we began to answer some basic questions we faced.

Start with an Inner-City Map

When we started, we made long lists of ways to serve our community's poor. Fix-it lists. Prescriptions for healing. A map to get out of poverty. Then somebody suggested we ask the *poor people* what they needed.

Somebody suggested we ask the *poor people* what they needed.

We did. One lady told us she wrapped empty boxes to put under the Christmas tree. We supplied her with Christmas toys. That experience eventually gave birth to an annual Christmas shop for children of our Life Skills Lab students.

Two others gave us a quick course on food stamps. We thought they could buy anything with this government currency. Not so! Mothers couldn't buy disposable diapers, deodorant, aspirin, or household cleaners. We opened a commodities closet to a regular clientele whose government aid left empty spaces in the household cabinets.

Several members of our congregation noticed that poor students came to school without pencils or paper. Hit by government cutbacks, these institutions faced problems trying to educate the poorest children in our city. Children within a mile of our church building struggled to learn without adequate equipment. We started to provide school supplies through a one-day "School Store," supplying over 55,000 children from 1990-1999.

Now we know. Before we take any step, before we lay any plan, before we start any new ministry, we first ask the people we plan to help. We've been delighted with the information we've received, with the relationships we've built, but more so with the hope we've revived. Living in the suburbs, we knew little about the actual conditions of people in poverty, but by talking with the poor, we overcame an information deficit.

We Needed a History Lesson

We haven't stopped learning. The three of us visited Dr. Ray Bakke in Chicago. He writes extensively and speaks internationally on urban ministry.[2] This esteemed expert lives in the inner city. His office is above a homeless shelter. He raised his family in a Chicago ghetto. Despite offers to move to other cities, Ray stays in Chicago because it's his city. As we toured the Windy City, he impressed us, not only with his commitment, but with his knowledge of Chicago. "You can't minister to a city you don't know," he said. He knew how Polish immigrants built houses. He pointed to the spot where Mrs. O'Leary's cow kicked over the lantern. He took us to an inner-city church of ten thousand members. He knew the history of Chicago. It was a convicting moment for the three of us.

We returned to Memphis determined to learn more about our city. The leaders of our ministries to the poor took a historical tour of Memphis. In the nineteenth century, the largest slave auction in America took place in Memphis. Memphian Robert Church was among the first black millionaires in America. We saw the corner where a white mob lynched a black man and the house where a white man risked his life to save black slaves. It all happened on our soil. It's part of our history. It's what brought us to this point.

With a greater understanding of the past, we now minister more adequately and more hopefully in the present. We see our efforts in a broader perspective. It helps us understand the reason behind the anger, the long history of oppression, and the barriers between the races. We want to know more about our city. We wish we'd learned earlier what we know now.

Ready? Get Set! Stop!

We've been confused, stumped, dumbfounded, and perplexed. We've approached decisions not knowing which way to turn. We've started with high hopes only to have them dashed along the way. We laid great plans that we later ignored. Through it all, we've learned never to minister without prayer. More than once, we've called Memphis churches to prayer and fasting. God answered with a ministry to a sizable group of people now changed by the gospel. Looking back ten years, we are amazed at how God has responded to our prayers.

Through it all, we've learned never to minister without prayer.

A Sunday afternoon meeting in the spring of 1989 ended in a big argument. We wanted to plant an inner-city church. Some demanded we start right away at the first available spot. Others insisted we study what others were doing and make a deliberate proposal. Tempers flared. We actually ended up doing both. Some began a study on the front porch of a nearby shotgun house, which brought a handful to Christ. Others wrote a proposal for starting an inner-city church, presenting the elders with a forty-page analysis of poverty in Memphis, discussions of similar efforts by other churches of Christ, and a plan for a church planting in two of the city's housing projects. Cleaborn and Foote Homes topped the list of possibilities.

Ready?

Get set!

Stop!

The church leaders mulled over the plan. The research seemed comprehensive. The efforts of others proved fruitful. The target area appeared open. Yet leadership hesitated.

We prayed again. We wondered if the plan was a good one. We worried about failure. Should we begin a ministry in Cleaborn and Foote Homes? A few weeks later, we got a letter from the President of the Resident's Council at Cleaborn Homes. We didn't know her. She knew nothing of our plans. She'd never read our report. She wasn't a church-going person. But she invited us to teach children about Jesus in a government-owned building in Cleaborn Homes, the exact project we'd targeted by our study!

Suddenly, the confusion vanished. It did for us. It will for you.

We remember. We've also learned. We know the questions most often asked about helping the poor because we've asked them. Through experience and the words of God, we now know some answers. As increasing numbers of those 350,000 congregations in America open their hearts toward the poor, we hope a little help from "seasoned" second graders will be a welcome gift.

---

1. Henry G. Cisneros, *Higher Ground* (Washington, DC: U.S. Dept. of H.U.D., 1996), p. 1.

2. See Ray Bakke, *The Urban Christian* (Downers Grove, IL: InterVarsity, 1987).

Chapter Twelve Action Plans

1. Go through a Bible concordance and read every passage that deals with the poor, widows, orphans, and the rich. Write down your insights and discuss them with friends.

2. Engage people in dialogues about what your church can reasonably accomplish in its benevolence outreach with your available resources and talents.

3. Identify the social workers and social services people in your congregation. Invite them to an open discussion of the needs of your community and how your church can get involved.

4. Get to know your city. Drive through its streets. All of them. Pray for various sections of your town.

5. Get started!

Supplemental Bibliography

Conn, Harvey M., ed. *Planting and Growing Urban Churches: From Dream to Reality*. Grand Rapids: Baker, 1997.

Green, Clifford J., ed. *Churches, Cities, and Human Community: Urban Ministry in the United States, 1945-1985*. Grand Rapids: Eerdmans, 1996.

Lupton, Robert. "A Theology of Geography." *Urban Mission* (Jun 1993): 60-61.

Magnuson, Norris. *Salvation in the Slums: Evangelical Social Work, 1865-1920*. Grand Rapids: Baker, 1977.

Olasky, Marvin. *The Tragedy of American Compassion*. Wheaton: Crossway, 1992.

Palen, J. John. *The Urban World*. New York: McGraw-Hill, 1992.

Pannell, William. *Evangelism from the Bottom Up*. Grand Rapids: Zondervan, 1992.

Perkins, John M. *Beyond Charity: The Call to Christian Community Development*. Grand Rapids: Baker, 1993.

Ratliff, Joe S., and Michael J. Cox. *Church Planting in the African-American Community*. Nashville: Broadman Press, 1993.

Ronsvalle, John and Sylvia. *The Poor Have Faces: Loving Your Neighbor in the 21st Century*. Grand Rapids: Baker, 1991.

Shank, Harold, and Wayne Reed. "A Challenge to Suburban Evangelical Churches: Theological Perspectives on Poverty in America." *Journal of Interdisciplinary Studies* 7.1/2 (1995): 119-134.

Sherman, Amy. *Restorers of Hope*. Wheaton: Crossway Books, 1997.

Sider, Ronald J. *One-Sided Christianity? Uniting the Church to Heal a Lost and Broken World*. Grand Rapids: Zondervan, 1993.

_____. *Rich Christians in an Age of Hunger*. 3rd ed. Dallas: Word, 1990.

Usry, Glenn, and Craig S. Keener. *Black Man's Religion*. Downers Grove, IL: InterVarsity, 1996.

Wood, Anthony. "Addressing the Legacy of Racism in the Church." *The Christian Chronicle* 58 (August, 1999): 18-19.

Resources for Ministry among the Poor

Christian Relief Fund. P.O. Box 19760, Amarillo, TX 79114. (800) 858-4038. *A ministry serving third world children sponsored by Churches of Christ.*

Christian Community Development Association. 3848 West Ogden Ave., Chicago, IL 60632. (312) 762-0994. *A coalition of interdenominational groups providing services to the poor.*

Evangelicals for Social Action. 10 Lancaster Ave., Philadelphia, PA 19151. (215) 645-9390. *Interdenominational organization of people interested in the poor.*

HopeWorks (Verlon Harp, Director). 1930 Union Ave., Memphis, TN 38104. (901) 272-3700. *A ministry that conducts a Life Skills Lab.*

Memphis Inner City Outreach, Inc. (Don Todd). Box 221041, Memphis, TN 38122. dstmico@pop.net. (901) 726-1821, 527-8701. *A ministry of Christian Churches to the inner city poor and homeless of Memphis.*

Nashville Inner City Church of Christ (Lydell Thomas). 185 Anthes Drive, Nashville, TN 37210. (615) 255-1726.

Urban Ministry Conference. Contact Anthony Wood. (901) 312-3486. mum92@aol.com. *A yearly conference on urban issues in Churches of Christ.*

Urban Ministry Studies, master's degree in Urban Ministry. Dr. Evertt Huffard. Harding Graduate School, 1000 Cherry Road, Memphis, TN 38117. ehuffard@hugsr.edu.

Urban Ministry Studies, master's degree in Urban Ministry. Contact Charlie Middlebrook. Imapct Church of Christ, 1704 Weber, Houston, TX 77007. (713) 370-8014.

About the Authors

Harold Shank

Harold Shank has served as one of the preaching ministers of the Highland Street Church of Christ in Memphis, Tennessee, since 1986.

Dr. Shank received his Ph.D. from Marquette University, M.A.R. and M.A. degrees from Harding Graduate School of Religion, and B.A. from Oklahoma Christian College.

He is a member of various organizations: the Steering Committee for Memphis Urban Ministry, National Spokesman for CCFSA, Secretary for Normal Business Alliance, Vice President of the University District, Inc., and Leadership Memphis. Some of Dr. Shank's articles have been published in *Leaven, 20ᵗʰ Century Christian, Christian Chronicle, Wineskins, Image, Power for Today, Restoration Quarterly*, and *21ˢᵗ Century Christian*. Among his published books are *Loosening Your Grip* and chapters in *Luke: A Gospel for the World; Where Genesis Meets Life; In Search of Wonder;* and *Theology Matters*.

He and his wife, Sally, have two sons, Daniel and Nathan, and live in Memphis.

Anthony Wood

Anthony Wood is Director of Memphis Urban Ministry with the Highland Street Church of Christ in Memphis, Tennessee, which starts churches among the poor and ethnic groups. Anthony and his family planted The Downtown Church in 1992. Anthony is a D.Min. candidate at Harding Graduate School of Religion, his M.Div. and M.A.R. are from Harding Graduate School of Religion, and he holds a B.A. from Harding University.

Mr. Wood has spoken at lectureships and conferences for Abilene Christian University, Harding University, Magnolia Bible College, Harding Graduate School of Religion, Southwestern Christian College, Mission/1000 Missionary Training Program, Urban Ministry Conference, Memphis Seminar, World Missions Workshop, Racial Reconciliation Workshop, and Herald of Truth Conference. Anthony is a member of the Steering Committee for Memphis Urban Ministry, Urban Ministry Conference National Steering Committee, Ukraine Executive Missions Committee, Highland St. Church City Missions Committee, and HopeWorks board..

His inner-city ministry articles have appeared in *Power for Today, Tri-State Christian Observer, Christian Chronicle,* and *21st Century Christian.* He contributed a chapter in the book edited by Allan Isom, *Touched by the Master.*

Anthony and his wife Candi have two teenagers, Seth and Naomi, and live in Memphis.

Ron Bergeron

Ron Bergeron serves as Family Life Counselor with the Southwest Church of Christ in Phoenix, Arizona. From 1988-1998, Ron served as Pastoral Counselor, Minister to Middle Adults, and Benevolence Minster at Highland Street Church of Christ and also as a therapist with HopeWorks in Memphis.

He received his M.Div. from Harding Graduate School of Religion and B.A. from North Carolina State University.

He has spoken for Urban Ministry Conference since 1989 and for the Herald of Truth Conference in 1998. Ron is a member of American Association for Marriage and Family Therapy, and a licensed Marriage and Family Therapist in Phoenix. He serves on the Memphis Greater Coalition for the Homeless, and the Steering Committee for Memphis Urban Ministry.

Ron and his wife Faith have two children, Natalie and Nicholas.